FIVE MINUTES
of
PEACE

FIVE MINUTES

of

PEACE

DAILY DEVOTIONS

365 Inspirations to Encourage Your Soul
Every Day of the Year

Includes previously published material from *Hugs Daily Inspirations*
Words of Comfort and *Hugs Daily Inspirations for Grandmas*

HOWARD BOOKS
NEW YORK   LONDON   TORONTO   SYDNEY   NEW DELHI

Howard Books
An Imprint of Simon & Schuster, Inc.
1230 Avenue of the Americas
New York, NY 10020

First Howard Books hardcover edition October 2018

HOWARD and colophon are trademarks of Simon & Schuster, Inc.

For information about special discounts for bulk purchases, please contact Simon & Schuster Special Sales at 1-866-506-1949 or business@simonandschuster.com.

The Simon & Schuster Speakers Bureau can bring authors to your live event. For more information or to book an event, contact the Simon & Schuster Speakers Bureau at 1-866-248-3049 or visit our website at www.simonspeakers.com.

Interior design by Davina Mock-Maniscalco

Manufactured in the United States of America

10 9 8 7 6 5 4 3 2 1

Library of Congress Cataloging-in-Publication Data is available.

ISBN 978-1-9821-0534-1
ISBN 978-1-9821-0535-8 (ebook)

There is a place of quiet rest. . . . There is a place of comfort sweet, near to the heart of God.

—Cleland B. McAfee

JANUARY

Finding Comfort in an Uncomfortable World

Peace I leave with you; My peace I give to you; not as the world gives do I give to you. Do not let your heart be troubled, nor let it be fearful.

JOHN 14:27 NASB

Sometimes the world can be an uncomfortable place. We may find ourselves rushing from point A to point Z with scarcely a moment to spare, all the while being bombarded by news that seems to signify imminent doom. How, then, can we find the assurance and comfort we so earnestly desire? By relying on God.

Today you are beginning a year of personal and spiritual growth. So as a gift to yourself, to your family, and to your friends, promise that you will do all within your power to seek and maintain the inner peace God gives. It is offered freely; it has been paid for in full; it is yours for the asking. So ask. And then share.

True contentment is a thing as active as agriculture.
It is the power of getting out of any situation all there is in it.

G. K. Chesterton

Faith Is the Answer

This is the victory that has overcome the world—our faith.

1 JOHN 5:4 NKJV

D o you desire the comfort, abundance, and victory God has promised? If so, you'll need to build a life that's founded upon faith: faith in your Creator, faith in yourself, faith in your family, and faith in the future. But sometimes finding and keeping faith can be difficult . . . and that's where God comes in.

If you place your life and your future in God's hands, He will reward you and guide your path. But if you try to rely only upon your own resources—if you seek to fly solo, without the assurance of your heavenly Father or the assistance of your loved ones—you're heading for trouble, and fast.

So today, make sure you do whatever is required to build your life upon a firm foundation of faith. Then, when you've entrusted your future to the Giver of all things good, rest assured that your future is secure, not only for today, but for all eternity.

Faith is the quiet place within us where we don't get whiplash every time life tosses us a curve.
Patsy Clairmont

An Attitude of Gratitude

Whatever is true, whatever is honorable,
whatever is just, whatever is pure, whatever is lovely,
whatever is commendable . . . dwell on these things.

PHILIPPIANS 4:8 HCSB

How will you direct your thoughts today? Will you follow the advice in Philippians 4:8 by dwelling on what is honorable, just, and commendable? Or will you let your thoughts be hijacked by the negativity that seems to dominate our troubled world? Are you fearful, angry, bored, or worried? Are you so preoccupied with the concerns of this day that you fail to thank God for the promise of eternity? Are you confused, bitter, or pessimistic? If so, God wants you to know He has better plans for you.

God wants you to experience a full and joyful life. So today, and every day hereafter, celebrate the life God has given you by focusing your thoughts on those things that are worthy of praise. Today, count your blessings instead of your hardships. And thank the Giver of all good things for His gifts, which are too numerous to count.

 The mind is like a clock that is constantly running down and must be wound up daily with good thoughts.

Fulton J. Sheen

Asking for Directions

If you need wisdom, ask our generous God, and he will
give it to you. He will not rebuke you for asking.

JAMES 1:5 NLT

Genuine, heartfelt prayer produces powerful changes in us and in our world. When we lift our hearts to God, we open ourselves to a never-ending source of divine wisdom and infinite love. Jesus made it clear to His disciples: they should petition God to meet their needs. So should we.

Do you have questions about your future that you simply can't answer? Do you have needs that you can't meet by yourself? Do you sincerely seek to know God's plan for your life? If so, ask Him for direction, for protection, and for strength—and then keep asking Him every day that you live. Whatever your need, no matter how great or small, pray about it and have faith. God is not just near; He is here, and He's perfectly capable of answering your prayers. It's up to you to ask.

You need not cry very loud;
He is nearer to us than we think.
Brother Lawrence

God Wants to Use You

*To everything there is a season, a time
for every purpose under heaven.*

ECCLESIASTES 3:1 NKJV

Each morning, as the sun rises in the east, you welcome a new day—one that is filled to the brim with opportunities, with possibilities, and with God. As you contemplate God's blessings in your own life, prayerfully seek His guidance for the day ahead.

Discovering God's unfolding purpose for your life is a daily journey, a pilgrimage guided by the teachings of God's holy Word. As you reflect upon His promises and upon the meaning those promises hold for you, ask God to lead you throughout the coming day. Let your heavenly Father direct your steps; concentrate on what God wants you to do now, and leave the distant future in hands that are far more capable than your own: His hands.

We aren't just thrown on this earth like dice tossed across a table. We are lovingly placed here for a purpose.
Charles Swindoll

This Is the Day

*I have spoken these things to you so that My joy
may be in you and your joy may be complete.*

JOHN 15:11 HCSB

God gives us this day; He fills it with possibilities, and He challenges us to use it for His purposes. Today, like every other day, is cause for celebration. This day is presented to us fresh and clean, free of charge, but we must remember that today is a nonrenewable resource—once it's gone, it's gone forever. Our responsibility is to use this day in the service of God and according to His will.

Treasure the day God has given you. Give Him the glory and the praise and the thanksgiving He deserves. And search for the hidden possibilities God has placed along your path. Today is a priceless gift from God, so use it joyfully, and encourage others to do the same. After all, as Psalm 118 tells us, this is the day the Lord has made. Rejoice and be glad in it!

*All our life is a celebration for us; we are convinced, in fact,
that God is always everywhere. We sing while we work . . .
we pray while we carry out all life's other occupations.*
Saint Clement of Alexandria

Your Highest Aspirations

You are my hope; O Lord God, You are my confidence.
PSALM 71:5 NASB

A re you willing to think big, to dream big, and to pray big? Are you willing to ask God to move mountains in your life, not just molehills? Are you an optimistic person who firmly believes that God is in control and that He protects people (like you) who honor and obey Him? If so, you are wise, and you are blessed.

Some people seem determined to keep their expectations in check, fearing that things won't work out and their hopes will be dashed. But when we choose not to expect the best from life—when we're too fearful or too pessimistic to hope for the best—we try to superimpose limitations on a God who has none.

So today, focus on your highest aspirations, and trust that God can help you achieve them . . . because He can. If it is in God's plan, it will come to pass.

Faith ought not to be a plaything.
If we believe, we should believe like giants.
Mary McLeod Bethune

The Power of Prayer

The intense prayer of the righteous is very powerful.

JAMES 5:16 CSB

The power of prayer: these words are familiar, yet sometimes we forget what they mean. Prayer helps us find strength for today and hope for the future. Prayer is not a thing to be taken lightly or to be used infrequently. God tells us in 1 Thessalonians 5 to pray continually. It is a powerful tool for communicating with our Creator, an opportunity to commune with the Giver of all good gifts.

The quality of your spiritual life will be in direct proportion to the quality of your prayer life. So today, instead of turning things over in your mind, turn them over to God in prayer. Instead of worrying about your next decision, ask God to lead the way. Pray constantly about things great and small. God is always listening, and He wants to hear from you now.

Where there is much prayer, there will be much of the Spirit; where there is much of the Spirit, there will be ever-increasing prayer.

Andrew Murray

Measuring Your Words

From a wise mind comes wise speech; the
words of the wise are persuasive.

PROVERBS 16:23 NLT

The words we speak are more important than we may realize. Our words have echoes that extend beyond place or time. If our words are encouraging, we can lift others up; if our words are hurtful, we can hold others back.

So here's a pair of questions for you to consider: Do you really try to be a source of encouragement to the people you encounter every day? And are you careful to speak words that lift those people up? If so, you will avoid angry outbursts. You will refrain from impulsive outpourings. You will terminate tantrums.

You will speak words of encouragement and hope to friends, to family members, to coworkers, and even to strangers. And by the way, all the aforementioned people have at least one thing in common: they, like just about everybody else in the world, need all the hope and encouragement they can get.

When someone does something good, applaud!
You will make two people happy.
Sam Goldwyn

The Fear Factor

Jesus immediately said to them:
"Take courage! It is I. Don't be afraid."
MATTHEW 14:27 NIV

The Book of Judges tells the story of Deborah, the fearless woman who helped lead the army of Israel to victory over the Canaanites. Deborah was a judge and a prophetess, a woman called by God to lead her people. And when she answered God's call, she was rewarded with one of the great victories of the Old Testament.

Like Deborah, all of us are called to serve our Creator. And we too may sometimes find ourselves facing trials that can bring trembling to the very depths of our souls. What should we do? We, like Deborah, should entrust our lives to God completely and without reservation. When we do, He gives us courage for today, hope for tomorrow, and joy for all eternity.

Courage is fear that has said its prayers.
Dorothy Bernard

Not Enough Hours?

It is good to give thanks to the Lord, to sing praises to the Most High. It is good to proclaim your unfailing love in the morning, your faithfulness in the evening.

PSALM 92:1–2 NLT

If you have too many demands and too few hours in which to meet them, you are in good company. Whether you're a young professional or a seasoned senior, it's easy to become overwhelmed from time to time.

What's a person to do? Well, you can start by making sure that you don't overcommit yourself (which means you'll probably need to start saying no a little more often). Next, you should tackle your responsibilities in the approximate order of their importance (first things first). Finally, after you've done your best, you should turn everything else over to your Creator.

You can be sure that God will give you the energy to do the most important things on today's to-do list if you ask Him. But remember that His "important" might not look like yours does. So ask Him . . . starting right now.

God calls us to seek Him daily in order to serve Him daily.
Sheila Cragg

God's Guidance

The Lord directs the steps of the godly. He
delights in every detail of their lives.

PSALM 37:23 NLT

God is intensely interested in your life, your faith, and your future. And He will guide your steps if you let Him. When you sincerely offer heartfelt prayers to your heavenly Father, He will give direction and meaning to your life. If you humbly seek His will, He will touch your heart and lead you on the path of His choosing.

When you entrust your life to Him completely, God will give you the strength to meet any challenge, the courage to face any trial, and the wisdom to live in His righteousness and in His peace. So trust Him today and seek His guidance. When you do, you can take each step with faith and confidence.

*A spiritual discipline is necessary in order to move slowly
from an absurd to an obedient life, from a life filled with
noisy worries to a life in which there is some free inner space
where we can listen to our God and follow His guidance.*
Henri Nouwen

Limitless Power, Limitless Love

I pray . . . that you may know the hope to which he has called
you . . . and his incomparably great power for us who believe.
EPHESIANS 1:18–19 NIV

When we worship God with faith and assurance, when we place Him at the absolute center of our lives, we invite His love into our hearts. In turn, we grow to love Him more deeply as we sense His love for us. Saint Augustine wrote, "I love You, Lord, not doubtingly, but with absolute certainty. Your Word beat upon my heart until I fell in love with You, and now the universe and everything in it tells me to love You."

Let us pray that we, too, will turn our hearts to the Creator, knowing with certainty that His heart has ample room for each of us and that we, in turn, must make room in our hearts for Him.

Our ways may seem good to us. We may even enjoy
some moderate successes. But when we do the work of
God in our own ways, we will never see the power of
God in what we do. God reveals His ways because
that is the only way to accomplish His purposes.
Henry Blackaby

When Opportunity Knocks

*Whatever you do, work at it with all your heart,
as working for the Lord, not for men.*

COLOSSIANS 3:23 NIV

In Matthew 25, Jesus tells a parable about a man who gives different amounts of money—talents—to three different servants while he's away. The two who go out into the world and use their talents are the ones who are rewarded by their master.

How are you using the talents that God has given you for His kingdom? Are you taking them out into the world and making the most of your opportunities? Or are you digging a hole in the ground and hiding your talent out of fear or thinking too little of yourself?

Today, pray that your eyes would be open to the opportunities that God gives you to share his love, his mercy, and your own talents. He's given them to you for a reason.

*Man's mind is not a container to be filled
but rather a fire to be kindled.*
Dorothea Brande

Look Up and Move On

*Let all bitterness, wrath, anger, clamor, and evil
speaking be put away from you, with all malice. And
be kind to one another, tenderhearted, forgiving one
another, even as God in Christ forgave you.*

EPHESIANS 4:31–32 NKJV

Are you wise enough to not be consumed with feelings of jealousy? The Bible clearly teaches us to love our neighbors, not to envy them. But sometimes, despite our best intentions, we fall prey to feelings of resentfulness, jealousy, bitterness, and envy. Why? Because we are human, and because we live in a world that places great importance on material possessions (possessions that, by the way, are totally unimportant to God).

So the next time you feel pangs of envy invading your thoughts, remind yourself of two things: (1) envy is wrong, and (2) God has already showered you with so many blessings that as a thoughtful, thankful person, you have no right to be envious of any other person on earth.

*Life appears to me too short to be spent in
nursing animosity, or registering wrongs.*
Charlotte Brontë

Finding Comfort Every Day

*Peace, peace to you, and peace to your
helpers! For your God helps you.*

1 Chronicles 12:18 nkjv

Comfort is a popular word in today's world. Marketers extol the value of comfortable clothes, comfortable shoes, comfortable furniture, comfortable cars, even "comfort foods." But despite advertisers' claims to the contrary, genuine comfort, the kind of inner peace and contentment we all desire, can't be purchased at a store. Lasting comfort begins in the heart . . . and comes from God.

Where do you go to find comfort? Are you seeking the kind of comfort the world promises but so often fails to deliver? Or are you seeking the inner peace and comfort that flows from the loving Creator of the universe?

Seek comfort in the arms of God, and He will give it to you.

*When I am criticized, injured, or afraid, there
is a Father who is ready to comfort me.*
Max Lucado

Finding Comfort in God's Promises

*Let's keep a firm grip on the promises that keep
us going. He always keeps his word.*

HEBREWS 10:23 MSG

God has given us a road map for our lives and our Christian faith, a love letter to each of us and a collection of the promises that He is sure to keep: the Bible. We are called upon to study its meaning, to trust its promises, to follow its instructions, and to share its good news. God's Word is a transforming, life-changing, one-of-a-kind treasure. A mere passing acquaintance with the Good Book is insufficient for those who seek to understand God and discern His Will.

God has made promises to you, and He intends to keep them. So take Him at His Word. Trust His promises, and share them with your family, with your friends, and with the world. Why not start today?

*God does not give us everything we want, but
He does fulfill His promises, leading us along
the best and straightest paths to Himself.*
Dietrich Bonhoeffer

The Cure for Guilt

If you hide your sins, you will not succeed. If you confess and reject them, you will receive mercy.

PROVERBS 28:13 NCV

All of us have made mistakes, and all of us have displeased God. Sometimes our sins have resulted from our own stubborn rebellion against God's commandments. And sometimes we go along with the crowd, leading us to make poor choices. Both can lead us to experience feelings of guilt. But God has an answer for the condemnation we feel: His grace. When we repent of our sins and ask God for forgiveness, He gives it. Period.

Are you troubled by feelings of guilt or regret? If so, ask God to forgive you. Take stock of your actions and stop doing the things you're not proud of. Finally, forgive yourself just as God has forgiven you—thoroughly, unconditionally, and immediately.

There is nothing, absolutely nothing, that God will not forgive. You cannot "out-sin" His forgiveness. You cannot "out-sin" the love of God.

Kathy Troccoli

Finding Happiness

Happy is the one . . . whose hope is in the Lord.
PSALM 146:5 HCSB

God intends that we should share His joy. In fact, the Bible teaches us that God's plan for our lives includes great joy, but our heavenly Father will not compel us to be joyful. We have to accept His joy (or reject it) ourselves.

Corrie ten Boom, who helped save almost eight hundred Jews during the Holocaust and survived a concentration camp herself, said this: "Happiness isn't something that depends on our surroundings . . . It's something we make inside ourselves."

God wants you to know true joy, but you must choose to accept the joy He offers. The way to do that is to meditate on and put your hope in Him. Today, direct your thoughts accordingly and you'll be looking in the right place for true happiness.

Happiness doesn't depend upon who you are or what you have; it depends upon what you think.
Dale Carnegie

More to Learn Every Day

There's something here also for seasoned men and
women, still a thing or two for the experienced to learn—
Fresh wisdom to probe and penetrate, the rhymes and
reasons of wise men and women. Start with God.

PROVERBS 1:5–7 MSG

No matter how old you are, God isn't finished with you yet, and He isn't finished teaching you important lessons about life here on earth and life eternal.

As a spiritual being, you have the potential to grow in your personal knowledge of the Lord every day that you live. You can do so through prayer, through worship, through an openness to God, and through a careful study of His Holy Word. Your Bible contains powerful prescriptions for everyday living. If you sincerely seek to walk with God, you should commit yourself to the thoughtful study of His teachings.

When you study God's Word and follow in the footsteps of His Son, you will become wise . . . and you will serve as a shining example to your friends, to your family, and to the world.

Today is yesterday's pupil.
Thomas Fuller

Infinite Possibilities

Is any thing too hard for the Lord?

GENESIS 18:14 KJV

Are you afraid to ask God to work miracles in your life? If so, it's time to abandon your doubts and to reclaim your faith in God's promises.

Our Creator is a God of infinite possibilities. Sometimes it seems like God is not all-powerful, or that He doesn't care to interfere in our world. But we cannot possibly fathom the workings of an infinite God with our finite minds.

God's Word makes it clear that absolutely nothing is impossible for the Lord. And since the Bible means what it says, you can be comforted in the knowledge that the Creator of the universe can do miraculous things in your life and in the lives of your loved ones. Your task is simple: to take God at His Word . . . and expect the miraculous.

God specializes in things thought impossible.
Catherine Marshall

Relying on God

Humble yourselves under the mighty hand of God,
that He may exalt you at the proper time, casting all
your anxiety on Him, because He cares for you.

1 Peter 5:6–7 nasb

Do the demands of this day threaten to overwhelm you? If so, take heart—and remember to rely not only on your own resources or on your family and friends, but also on the promises of your Father in heaven.

God is a never-ending source of support and courage for those who call on Him. When we are weary, He gives us strength. When we see no hope, God reminds us of His promises. When we grieve, God comforts us.

God will hold your hand and walk with you every day of your life if you let Him. So even when your circumstances are difficult, trust the Father. His love is eternal, and His goodness endures forever.

*Faith is not merely you holding on to God—
it is God holding on to you.*
E. Stanley Jones

Growing with God

*Every morning he wakes me. He teaches me to listen
like a student. The Lord God helps me learn.*

Isaiah 50:4–5 NCV

Each new day is a gift from God, so we would be wise to spend a few quiet moments each morning thanking the Giver. Daily life is woven with the threads of habit, and no habit is more important to our spiritual health than the discipline of daily prayer and devotion to the Creator.

When we begin each day with our heads bowed and our hearts lifted, we remind ourselves of God's love, His protection, and His commandments. And if we are wise, we align our priorities for the coming day with the teachings and commandments that God has given us through His Holy Word.

Are you seeking to change some aspect of your life? Then take time out of your hectic schedule to spend time each day with your Creator. Do you seek to improve the condition of your spiritual or physical health? If so, ask for God's help, and ask for it many times each day . . . starting with your morning devotional.

*If [you] desire to profit, read with humility,
simplicity, and faithfulness.*
Thomas à Kempis

Honoring God

Honor God with everything you own; give him the first and
the best. Your barns will burst, your wine vats will brim over.

PROVERBS 3:9 MSG

A moment's peace can be a scarce commodity. But no matter
how numerous the interruptions and demands of the day,
God is ever-present, always ready and willing to offer solace to
those who seek "the peace that passes all understanding."

Whom will you choose to honor today? If you honor God
and place Him at the center of your life, every day is a cause for
celebration.

Honor God for who He is and for what He has done for
you. And don't just honor Him on Sunday morning. Praise
Him all day, every day, for as long as you live . . . and then for
all eternity.

God shows unbridled delight when He sees
people acting in ways that honor Him.
Bill Hybels

Live Your Life

What a gift life is to those who stay the course! You've heard, of course, of Job's staying power, and you know how God brought it all together for him at the end. That's because God cares, cares right down to the last detail.

JAMES 5:11 MSG

"The thief comes only to steal and kill and destroy," says Jesus in John 10:10. "I came that they may have life and have it abundantly."

What does it look like to live a life abundantly? God doesn't promise us material abundance—a big house, a high-paying job, or the things this world hails as "successful." But he has promised us a life filled with love, filled with joy, and filled with His incredible, life-giving presence.

Be faithful with what God gives you, and stay the course even through rejection and heartache. And get busy. Because it's your life, and the living is up to you.

I have held many things in my hands, and have lost them all; but whatever I have placed in God's hands, that I still possess.
Martin Luther

Forgiving and Forgetting

Real wisdom, God's wisdom, begins with a holy life and is characterized by getting along with others. It is gentle and reasonable, overflowing with mercy and blessings.

JAMES 3:17 MSG

Most of us find it difficult to forgive the people who have hurt us. And that's too bad, because life would be much simpler if we could forgive people "once and for all" and be done with it. But forgiveness is seldom that easy. Usually the decision to forgive is straightforward; it's the process of forgiving that's more difficult. Forgiveness is a journey that requires time, perseverance, and prayer.

If you sincerely wish to forgive someone, pray for that person—and keep praying. While you're at it, pray for yourself, too, asking God to heal your heart. Don't expect forgiveness to be easy or instantaneous, but rest assured that with God as your partner, you can forgive and enjoy a life of peace with those around you.

 In this life, if you have anything to pardon, pardon quickly. Slow forgiveness is little better than no forgiveness.
Arthur Wing Pinero

Learning from Mistakes

I waited patiently for the Lord; he turned to me and heard my cry. He lifted me out of the slimy pit, out of the mud and mire; he set my feet on a rock and gave me a firm place to stand. He put a new song in my mouth, a hymn of praise to our God.

PSALM 40:1–3 NIV

Life can be a struggle at times. And everybody (including you) makes mistakes. But our goal should be to make them only once.

Have you experienced a recent setback? If so, look for the lesson God is trying to teach you. Instead of complaining about life's sad state of affairs, learn what needs to be learned, change what needs to be changed, and move on. View failure as an opportunity to realign your life with God's will. View disappointment as opportunities to learn more about yourself and your world.

The next time you make one of life's inevitable blunders, choose to turn your misstep into a stepping-stone. Then step right past failure to success.

Being human means you will make mistakes. And you will make mistakes, because failure is God's way of moving you in another direction.
Oprah Winfrey

Finding Comfort
Outside Your Comfort Zone

The Lord is my light and my salvation; whom shall I fear? The Lord is the strength of my life; of whom shall I be afraid?

PSALM 27:1 NKJV

Have you spent too much time playing it safe? Are you uncomfortably stuck inside your comfort zone? Would you like to change the quality and direction of your life, but you're not sure how? If you answered these questions in the affirmative, maybe you're more afraid of change than you need to be.

Change is often difficult and sometimes uncomfortable. But the world keeps changing, and the longer you delay needed changes, the more painful they'll become. Instead of fighting change, maybe it's time to embrace it.

The next time you face a decision that involves a major modification in your own circumstances, look to God. He will give you the courage to step outside your comfort zone.

You gain strength, courage, and confidence by every experience in which you really stop to look fear in the face. You are able to say to yourself, "I lived through this horror. I can take the next thing that comes along." You must do the things you think you cannot do.

Eleanor Roosevelt

Thanksgiving, Yes . . . Envy, No!

A heart at peace gives life to the body, but envy rots the bones.
PSALM 14:30 NIV

As the recipient of God's grace, you have every reason to celebrate life. After all, God has promised you the opportunity to receive His abundance and His joy. But if you allow envy to gnaw away at the fabric of your soul, you'll find that joy remains elusive. When you're envious of others, you unintentionally rob yourself of the comfort and peace that might otherwise be yours.

So do yourself an enormous favor: rather than succumbing to envy, focus on the marvelous things God has done for you. Thank the Giver of all good gifts, and keep thanking Him for the wonders of His love and the miracles of His creation. Count your own blessings, and let your neighbors count theirs. It's a happier way to live.

You can't be envious and happy at the same time.
Frank Tyger

Your Unique Gifts

God has given each of you a gift from his great variety
of spiritual gifts. Use them well to serve one another.

1 PETER 4:10 NLT

Each of us possesses special talents, given to us by God, that can be nurtured or ignored. Our challenge is to use those abilities to the greatest extent possible—and to use them in ways that honor our Creator.

Are you using your talents to make the world a better place? If so, keep up the good work! But perhaps you have gifts that you haven't fully explored and developed. Why not have a chat today with the One who gave you those gifts? Your talents are priceless treasures bestowed on you by your heavenly Father. Use them. After all, the best way to say thank you to the Giver is to use what He has given.

*God has given you special talents—now it's
your turn to give them back to God.*
Marie T. Freeman

Where Is God Leading?

When troubles come your way, consider it an opportunity for great joy. For . . . when your faith is tested, your endurance has a chance to grow. So let it grow, for when your endurance is fully developed, you will be perfect and complete, needing nothing.

JAMES 1:2–4 NLT

Whether we realize it or not, times of adversity can be times of intense personal and spiritual growth. Our difficult days are also times when we can learn (or relearn) some of life's most important lessons.

The next time you experience a difficult moment, a difficult day, or even a difficult year, ask yourself this question: Where is God leading me? In times of struggle and sorrow, you can take comfort in knowing that God is leading you to a place of His choosing. Your duty is to watch, to pray, to listen, and to follow.

It is only because of problems that we grow mentally and spiritually.
M. Scott Peck

FEBRUARY

No Need to Worry

*Trust in him at all times, O people; pour out
your hearts to him, for God is our refuge.*

PSALM 62:8 NIV

In the game of life, you win some and you lose some. We live in an uncertain world, a world in which trouble may come calling at any moment. No wonder we may find ourselves feeling a little panicky at times.

Do you sometimes spend more time worrying about a problem than you spend solving it? If so, here's a strategy for dealing with your worries: take them to God. Take your troubles to Him; take your fears to Him; take your doubts to Him; take your weaknesses to Him; take your sorrows to Him . . . and leave them all there.

God is the Rock that cannot be moved. When you build your life upon that Rock, you have absolutely no need to worry . . . not now, not ever.

*When God is at the center of your life,
you worship, when He's not, you worry.*
Rick Warren

God's Guidebook

Every word of God is flawless;
he is a shield to those who take refuge in him.

PROVERBS 30:5 NIV

Do you read your Bible a lot . . . or not? The answer to this simple question will determine, to a surprising extent, the quality of your life and of your faith.

As you establish priorities for life, you must choose whether God's Word will be the bright spotlight that guides your path each day or a tiny night-light that occasionally provides a flicker in the dark. The decision to study the Bible—or not to—is yours and yours alone. But make no mistake: how you choose to use your Bible will have a profound impact on you and your loved ones.

The Bible is the ultimate guide for life; make it your personal guidebook as well. God's message has the power to transform your day . . . and your life.

Reading news without reading the Bible will inevitably lead to an unbalanced life, an anxious spirit, a worried and depressed soul.
Bill Bright

Too Much Busyness, too Little Peace

*Those who love your instructions have
great peace and do not stumble.*

PSALM 119:165 NLT

Has the hectic pace of life robbed you of the peace that might otherwise be yours? Do you sometimes find yourself overcommitted and underprepared? Are you too busy for your own good? If so, it's probably time to slow down long enough to reorganize your day and reorder your priorities.

God offers every human being (including you) a peace that surpasses mortal understanding; but He doesn't force anyone (including you) to accept it. God's peace is freely offered but not mandated.

Today, as a gift to yourself, to your family, and to the world, be still and experience God's presence. Open your heart to His love. Claim the genuine peace that can be yours for the asking. And then share that blessing and comfort with those around you.

*Often our lives are strangled by things
that don't ultimately matter.*
Grady Nutt

Always with Us

*A child is born to us, a son is given to us. The government
will rest on his shoulders. And he will be called: Wonderful
Counselor, Mighty God, Everlasting Father, Prince of Peace.*

ISAIAH 9:6 NLT

Are you facing difficult circumstances or unwelcome changes? If so, you can take comfort in knowing that God is far bigger than any problem you may face. So instead of worrying about life's inevitable challenges, put your faith in the Father and His only Son: "Jesus Christ is the same yesterday, today, and forever" (Hebrews 13:8 NKJV). It is precisely because God does not change that you can face your challenges with courage for today and hope for tomorrow.

Life is often trying, but you need not be fearful. God loves you, and He will protect you. In times of hardship, He will comfort you; in times of change, He will guide your path. When you're troubled or weak or sorrowful, God is always with you. Build your life on your Rock, your Fortress, and your Deliverer. God doesn't change. Because He's always with you, you can always trust Him.

*It is a joy that God never abandons His children.
He guides faithfully all who listen to His directions.*

Corrie ten Boom

Quality Time

Teach us to number our days, that we
may gain a heart of wisdom.

PSALM 90:12 NKJV

You've probably heard about the difference between "quality time" and "quantity time." Your family and friends need both. So as a responsible member of a loving family, you'll want to invest large quantities of time and energy in the care and nurturing of your clan.

But is your life so busy and your to-do list so full that you scarcely have a moment to spare? Does it seem you can never find quite enough time to spend with the people you care about? If so, today is a good day to begin rearranging your priorities and your life. And while you're at it, make sure God remains squarely at the center of your heart. When you do, He will bless you and yours in ways you could have scarcely imagined.

*If I were starting my family over again, I would give
first priority to my wife and children, not to my work.*
Richard Halverson

Finding Comfort in Church

*If two or three people come together in
my name, I am there with them.*

MATTHEW 18:20 NCV

In the Book of Acts, Luke reminds us to "be like shepherds to the church of God" (Acts 20:28 ICB). And what was appropriate in New Testament times is equally true today. We'll be wise to honor God not only in our hearts but also in our houses of worship.

Do you feed your soul by feeding the church of God? Do you attend regularly and are you an active participant? We can't carry out the journey of life and faith on our own; we need to love others and be loved in return, the way God loves.

So do yourself a favor—become actively involved in your church. Don't just go to services out of habit. Join out of a sincere desire to know and worship God. When you do, you'll be blessed by the One who sent His Son to die so that you might have everlasting life.

*The church is not an end in itself; it is a means
to the end of the kingdom of God.*
E. Stanley Jones

The Voice Inside Your Head

I strive always to keep my conscience clear before God and man.
ACTS 24:16 NIV

Your conscience is an early warning system designed by God to keep you out of trouble. Whenever you're about to make a significant error in judgment, that little voice inside your head has a way of speaking up. If you listen to God as He speaks through your conscience, you'll be wise; if you ignore Him, you'll be putting yourself at risk.

Whenever you're about to make an important decision, listen carefully to God's quiet voice as He whispers in your heart and mind. Sometimes, you would rather drown out that voice and go your own way. From time to time, you'll be tempted to abandon your better judgment. But remember that a conscience is a terrible thing to waste. So instead of ignoring that quiet little voice, pay careful attention to it. Be sure it's tuned in to God's Spirit and in line with His Word. If you do, you'll be led in the right direction. In fact, God wants to lead you right now. Listen to His voice.

Your conscience is your alarm system. It's your protection.
Charles Stanley

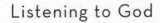

Listening to God

Listen in silence before me.
ISAIAH 41:1 NLT

When we petition God, He responds. God's hand is not absent, and it is not distant. It is responsive.

On his second missionary journey, Paul started a small church in Thessalonica. A short time later, he penned a letter that was intended to encourage the new believers at that church. Today, almost two thousand years later, 1 Thessalonians remains a powerful, practical guide for Christian living.

In his letter, Paul advises members of the new church to "pray without ceasing." His advice applies to Christians of every generation, including our own. When we weave the habit of prayer into the very fabric of our days, we invite God to become a partner in every aspect of our lives. When we consult God on an hourly basis, we avail ourselves of His wisdom, His strength, and His love.

God doesn't usually send His messages on stone tablets or post them on city billboards. He communicates in subtler ways. If you sincerely desire to hear His voice, you must set aside time to create a quiet, willing place in your heart—and listen.

Half an hour of listening is essential except when one is very busy. Then, a full hour is needed.
Saint Francis de Sales

No Complaints

*Do everything without complaining or arguing. Then
you will be innocent and without any wrong.*

PHILIPPIANS 2:14–15 NCV

Most of us have more blessings than we can count, yet we still find reasons to complain about the minor frustrations of everyday life. To do so, of course, is not only shortsighted, it's also a serious roadblock on the path to spiritual abundance.

Would you like to feel more comfortable about your circumstances and your life? Then be determined to do whatever it takes to ensure that you focus your thoughts and energy on the major blessings you've received (not the minor inconveniences you must occasionally endure).

The next time you're tempted to gripe about the frustrations of everyday living, don't do it! Today and every day, make it a practice to count your blessings, not your hardships. It's a much more joyful way to live.

*Life is too short to nurse one's misery.
Hurry across the lowlands so that you may
spend more time on the mountaintops.*
Phillips Brooks

Beyond Mediocrity

Do not lack diligence; be fervent in spirit; serve the Lord.

ROMANS 12:11 HCSB

God expects us to conduct ourselves with dignity and discipline. The Bible reminds us again and again that our Creator intends for us to lead disciplined lives—and we should take God at His Word, despite the temptation to take the easy way out.

We live in a world in which leisure is glorified and indifference is often glamorized. But God did not create us for lives of mediocrity; He created us for His kingdom.

Life's greatest rewards seldom fall into our laps; to the contrary, our greatest accomplishments usually require lots of work. But God has given us each an adequate measure of strength and ability. He knows we're up to the tasks He sends our way, and He has big plans for us; may we, as disciplined followers of God, always be worthy of those plans.

No horse gets anywhere until he is harnessed. . . . No life ever grows great until it is focused, dedicated, disciplined.
Harry Emerson Fosdick

Your Marathon Partner

Don't look for shortcuts to God. The market is flooded with surefire, easygoing formulas for a successful life that can be practiced in your spare time. Don't fall for that stuff, even though crowds of people do. The way to life—to God!—is vigorous and requires total attention.

MATTHEW 7:13–14 MSG

As we all know, hope can be a perishable commodity. Despite God's promises, and despite our countless blessings, we are frail and fearful human beings, and we can still lose hope from time to time. When we do, we need the encouragement of close friends and family members, and we need the healing touch of God's hand.

Even though this world can be a place of trials and struggles, God has promised us peace, joy, and eternal life if we entrust our lives to Him. So today, as you face the challenges and obligations of everyday life, work as if everything depended upon you, but pray as if everything depended upon God. Then, when you've done your best, you can trust God to do the rest.

We ought to make some progress, however little, every day, and show some increase of fervor. We ought to act as if we were at war—as, indeed, we are—and never relax until we have won the victory.
Saint Teresa of Avila

Imaginary Problems

Jesus said, "Don't let your hearts be troubled.
Trust in God, and trust in me."

JOHN 14:1 NCV

In the golden age of television, Steve Allen shaped the sleeping habits of millions of Americans with his program, *The Tonight Show*. Steve was one of the most versatile and influential entertainers of the twentieth century. But did he ever lose sleep over the many problems associated with live television? Hardly. He said, "One of the nice things about problems is that a good many of them do not exist except in our own imaginations." And he was right.

The next time you find yourself dreading some vaguely defined future event, remember Steve Allen's observation and quit fretting. As Steve indicated, many of our problems are imaginary. And when it comes to facing those that aren't, trusting in God beats worry tonight and every night.

*I am an old man and have known a great many
troubles, but most of them never happened.*
Mark Twain

Do It Now

Remember this: the person who sows sparingly
will also reap sparingly, and the person who sows
generously will also reap generously.

2 CORINTHIANS 9:6 HCSB

If you'd like another simple prescription for finding—and keeping—happiness, here it is: learn to do first things first, and learn to do them sooner rather than later.

Are you in the habit of doing what needs to be done when it needs to be done, or are you a dues-paying member of the Procrastinators' Club? If you've acquired the habit of doing your most important work first, congratulations! But if you find yourself putting off all those unpleasant tasks until later (or never), it's time to think about the consequences of your behavior.

You can free yourself from the emotional quicksand by paying less attention to your fears and more attention to your responsibilities. So when you're faced with an unpleasant responsibility, don't spend endless hours fretting over it. Simply seek God's counsel and get busy. When you do, you will be richly rewarded because of your willingness to act.

Action breeds confidence and courage. If you want to conquer fear, do not sit home and think about it. Go out and get busy.
Dale Carnegie

The Foundations of Family Ties and Friendships

Putting away lying, "Let each one of you speak truth with his neighbor," for we are members of one another.

EPHESIANS 4:25 NKJV

Family ties and lasting friendships are built upon a foundation of honesty and trust. It has been said on many occasions that honesty is the best policy. Yet it is far more important to note that honesty is God's policy.

Sometimes honesty is difficult; sometimes honesty is painful; sometimes honesty makes us feel uncomfortable. Despite these temporary feelings of discomfort, we must make honesty the hallmark of all our relationships; otherwise, we invite needless suffering into our own lives and into the lives of those we love.

Sometime soon, perhaps even today, you will be tempted to bend the truth. Resist that temptation. Truth is God's way. Always make it your way, too.

The single most important element in any human relationship is honesty—with oneself, with God, and with others.
Catherine Marshall

Worshipping God Every Day

An hour is coming, and is now here, when the true worshipers
will worship the Father in spirit and truth. Yes, the Father
wants such people to worship Him. God is Spirit, and those
who worship Him must worship in spirit and truth.

JOHN 4:23–24 HCSB

I f you genuinely desire to receive God's comfort, you must be
willing to worship Him not just on Sunday, but on every day
of the week. God has a wonderful plan for your life, and an
important part of that plan includes the time you set aside for
praise and worship.

Every life, including yours, includes some form of worship.
The question is not whether you will worship, but what you
worship. If you choose to worship God, you'll reap a bountiful
harvest of joy, peace, and abundant blessing. So do yourself
this favor: Worship God with sincerity and thanksgiving today
and every day. Write His name on your heart—and rest assured that your name is written on His.

*If you will not worship God seven days a week,
you do not really worship Him on one day a week.*
A. W. Tozer

First Place

Fear of the Lord is the foundation of true wisdom.
All who obey his commandments will grow in wisdom.

PSALM 111:10 NLT

If you really want to know God, you can start by putting Him first in your life. So here's a question worth thinking about: Have you made God your top priority by offering Him your heart, your soul, your talents, and your time? Or are you in the habit of giving God little more than a few hours on Sunday morning? The answers to these questions will greatly affect the quality of your life and the content of your character.

Some folks choose to worship God and, as a result, receive the joy He offers to His children. Other folks seem determined to do things their way, with decidedly mixed results. Which kind of person are you? Does God rule your heart? If you sincerely want to know Him, you must answer yes—you must put your Creator in first place.

You must ask for God's help. . . . After each failure,
ask forgiveness, pick yourself up, and try again.
C. S. Lewis

Richly Blessed

God loves a cheerful giver.

2 CORINTHIANS 9:7 NIV

A re you a cheerful giver? If you follow the instruction in God's Word, you must be. When we give, God looks not only at the quality of our gift, but also at the condition of our heart. If we give generously, joyfully, and without complaint, we'll be living in accordance with God's plan. But if we offer our gifts grudgingly, or if our motivation for giving is selfish, our generosity will fall short of pleasing our Creator—even if our gift is a generous one.

Today, pledge to be a cheerful, generous, courageous giver. The world needs your help, and you'll benefit from the spiritual rewards that will be yours when you give faithfully, prayerfully, and cheerfully.

The mind grows by taking in,
but the heart grows by giving out.
Warren Wiersbe

Embracing the Aging Process

*Gray hair is a glorious crown; it is found
in the way of righteousness.*

PROVERBS 16:31 HCSB

We live in a society that glorifies youth. The messages that we receive from the media are unrelenting: we are told that we must do everything within our power to retain youthful values and a youthful appearance. The goal, we are told, is to remain "forever young"—yet this goal is not only unrealistic, but it is also unworthy of men and women who understand what genuine beauty is, and what it isn't.

When it comes to health and beauty, you should focus more on health than on beauty. In fact, when you take care of your physical, spiritual, and mental health, your appearance will tend to take care of itself. And remember: God loves you during every stage of life. So embrace the aging process for what it is: an opportunity to grow closer to your loved ones and to your Creator.

It is magnificent to grow old, if one keeps young.
Harry Emerson Fosdick

God Is Available

Where can I go from your Spirit? Where can I flee from your presence? If I go up to the heavens, you are there; if I make my bed in the depths, you are there. If I rise on the wings of the dawn, if I settle on the far side of the sea, even there your hand will guide me, your right hand will hold me fast.

PSALM 139:7–10 NIV

If God is everywhere, why does He sometimes seem so far away? The answer to that question really has nothing to do with God; it has to do with us—how we think, how we worship, and how we choose to spend our time.

When we begin each day on our knees, in praise and worship, God often seems near indeed. But if we ignore God's presence or, worse yet, rebel against it altogether, the world in which we live becomes spiritually barren.

Today, and every day, praise God. Wherever you are—whether you're energized or exhausted, happy or sad, victorious or vanquished—celebrate God's presence. Be comforted, for He is here.

There is nothing more important in any life than the constantly enjoyed presence of the Lord. . . . for without it we shall make mistakes, and without it we shall be defeated.
Alan Redpath

His Intimate Love

As the Father loved Me,
I also have loved you; abide in My love.

JOHN 15:9 NKJV

D o you seek an intimate, one-on-one relationship with your heavenly Father, or are you satisfied to keep Him at a "safe" distance? Saint Augustine once said, "God loves each of us as if there were only one of us." Do you believe those words?

Even on those difficult days when God seems distant—or even absent—you can be sure that His love for you remains unchanged. He knows every thought, He watches every step, and He hears every prayer. Today and every day, your loving, heavenly Father is waiting patiently for you to reach out to Him. So open your heart to God. You can trust Him and abide in His love without fear and without reservation, because you are His precious child.

*God does not love us because we are valuable.
We are valuable because God loves us.*
Fulton J. Sheen

Secure in His Hands

*Be of good courage, and He shall strengthen
your heart, all you who hope in the Lord.*

PSALM 31:24 NKJV

Open your Bible to its center, and you'll find the book of Psalms. In it are some of the loveliest words ever translated into the English language. One of the most beautiful is Psalm 23, in which David describes God as a shepherd who cares for His flock.

You are God's priceless creation, made in His image, and protected by Him. God watches over every step you make and every breath you take, so you need never be afraid.

But fear has a way of slipping into the hearts of even the most faith filled. You'll confront circumstances that shake you to the core of your soul. When you're afraid, trust in God. When you're worried, turn your concerns over to Him. When you're anxious, remember the quiet assurance of God's promises. And then place your life in His care. You are secure in His hands.

*Entrust yourself entirely to God. He is a Father and a most
loving Father at that, who would rather let heaven and
earth collapse than abandon anyone who trusted in Him.*
Paul of the Cross

Becoming Wise

He who walks with the wise grows wise.

PROVERBS 13:20 NIV

Wisdom doesn't spring up overnight—it takes time. To become wise, we must seek God's wisdom and live according to His Word. And we must not only learn the lessons God teaches, but also live by them.

Would you like to experience the comfort and peace that results from a wisely lived life? If so, study the ultimate source of wisdom: the Word of God. Seek out worthy mentors and listen carefully to their advice. Associate, day in and day out, with mature, thoughtful friends. And act in accordance with God's wisdom and guidance gleaned through those resources. When you do these things, you will become wise . . . and you'll be a blessing to your friends, to your family, and to the world.

The process of living seems to consist in coming to realise truths so ancient and simple that, if stated, they sound like barren platitudes. They cannot sound otherwise to those who have not had the relevant experience: that is why there is no real teaching of such truths possible and every generation starts from scratch.

C. S. Lewis

Finding Work You Love

He did it with all his heart. So he prospered.

2 CHRONICLES 31:21 NKJV

Comedian George Burns found the secret to his own success, offering this advice: "fall in love with what you do for a living."

It's a simple phrase, but it's no easy task. Few people are lucky enough to discover the place where their passion meets their skillset, and even fewer are able to do it for a living.

This doesn't mean that we should stop looking, though. When you pray to God today, ask Him to guide you. Think about the things that you do to bring glory to Him, peace to others, and passion to your own life. Worship God in your work—in the parts that make your heart sing, but also in the drudgery of the everyday.

And whatever you do, do it for the Lord.

Never work just for money or for power.
They won't save your soul or help you sleep at night.
Marian Wright Edelman

The Right Kind of Leaders

*A good leader plans to do good, and those
good things make him a good leader.*

ISAIAH 32:8 NCV

Our world needs the right kind of leaders—leaders who are willing to honor God with their words and their deeds. But the same is true for your little corner of the world, too: your family and friends need people who are willing to lead by example, not merely by proclamation.

If you want to be the right kind of leader, begin by serving as a positive role model to those around you. After all, your words of instruction will never ring true unless you yourself are willing to follow them.

In fact, since good leaders are a rare treasure, the people in your life need you very much. Are you the kind of leader you would want to follow? Make that your goal today.

Leadership is the ability to lift and inspire.
Paul Dietzel

Beyond the Temptations

Friend, don't go along with evil. Model the good. The person who does good does God's work. The person who does evil falsifies God, doesn't know the first thing about God.

3 JOHN 1:11 MSG

We are all born into a world that tries its hardest to push us away from God's will. Society, it seems, is causing pain and heartache in more ways than ever before. We must remain watchful and strong. And the good news is this: when it comes to fighting evil, we are never alone. God is always with us, and He gives us the power to resist temptation whenever we ask Him to give us strength.

In a letter to believers, Peter offered a stern warning: "Your adversary, the devil, prowls around like a roaring lion, seeking someone to devour" (1 Peter 5:8 NASB). As a thoughtful person, you will take that warning seriously and encourage your loved ones to take it seriously, too.

In the Garden of Gethsemane, Jesus went through agony of soul in His efforts to resist the temptation to do what He felt like doing rather than what He knew was God's will for Him.

Joyce Meyer

Living on Purpose

In Him we were also made His inheritance, predestined
according to the purpose of the One who works out
everything in agreement with the decision of His will.

Ephesians 1:11 hcsb

Whenever we struggle against God's plans, we suffer.
When we resist God's calling, our efforts bear little
fruit. Our best strategy, therefore, is to seek God's wisdom and
to follow Him wherever He leads us.

God has a plan for your life. If you seek that plan sincerely
and prayerfully, you will find it. When you discover God's purpose for your life, you'll experience abundant blessing, peace,
comfort, and power—God's power. And that's the only kind
worth having.

*Be patient. God is using today's difficulties to strengthen
you for tomorrow. He is equipping you. The God
who makes things grow will help you bear fruit.*
Max Lucado

The Role Our Possessions Should Play

*Keep your lives free from the love of money,
and be satisfied with what you have.*

HEBREWS 13:5 NCV

On the grand stage of a well-lived life, material possessions should play a rather small role. Yet sometimes we allow our possessions to assume undue control over our lives. But God has a better plot for our lives, if we'll allow Him to be the director.

How much of your life are you investing in the pursuit of money and the things money can buy? Do you own your possessions, or are they starting to own more and more of you? Is your life ruled by the quest for riches of an earthly kind or of a spiritual kind?

If material possessions are ruling your life, take careful inventory and rid yourself of the overstock. After all, nothing on earth is valuable enough to allow it to separate you from your Creator.

*Theirs is an endless road, a hopeless maze, who
seek for goods before they seek for God.*
Saint Bernard of Clairvaux

The Importance of Praise

I will praise You with my whole heart.

<small>PSALM 138:1 NKJV</small>

Life is demanding, and most of us are busy indeed. Sometimes we allow ourselves to become so preoccupied with the demands of daily life that we forget to say thank you to the very One who gives us that life. But the Bible makes it clear, given how often praising God is mentioned, that praise is a vital part of our relationship with God.

Because God is always with us, and because He is always blessing us, worship and praise can—and should—become a part of everything we do. Otherwise, we can quickly lose perspective as we fall prey to the demands of the moment.

Do you sincerely wish to have close fellowship with the One who has given you eternal love and eternal life? Then praise Him today—and every day—for who He is and for all the wonderful things He has done for you.

*The Bible instructs—and experience teaches—
that praising God results in our burdens
being lifted and our joys being multiplied.*
Jim Gallery

MARCH

Conquering Everyday Frustrations

A hot-tempered man stirs up dissension,
but a patient man calms a quarrel.
PROVERBS 15:18 NIV

Life is full of frustrations, some great and some small.

On occasion you—like Jesus when He confronted the money changers in the temple—will confront evil with righteous anger. When you do, you may respond as He did— vigorously and without reservation.

But more often your frustrations will be of the comparatively mundane variety. As long as you live here on earth, you will face countless opportunities to lose your temper over small, relatively insignificant events: a traffic jam, a spilled cup of coffee, an inconsiderate comment. When you're tempted to lose your temper over the minor inconveniences of life, don't. Turn away from anger, hatred, bitterness, and regret. Turn instead to God and find comfort in Him.

When you strike out in anger, you may miss the
other person, but you will always hit yourself.
Jim Gallery

What to Do?

The lines of purpose in your lives never grow slack, tightly tied as they are to your future in heaven, kept taut by hope.

COLOSSIANS 1:5 MSG

What on earth does God intend for me to do with the rest of my life?" It's an easy question to ask but, for many of us, a difficult question to answer. Why? Because God's purposes aren't always clear to us. Sometimes we wander aimlessly in a wilderness of our own making. And sometimes we struggle mightily against God in an unsuccessful attempt to find success and happiness through our own means, not His.

Sometimes God's intentions will be clear to you; other times God's plan will seem uncertain at best. But even on those difficult days when you are unsure which way to turn, you must never lose sight of these overriding facts: God created you for a reason; He has important work for you to do; and He's waiting patiently for you to do it.

The next step is up to you.

It's incredible to realize that what we do each day has meaning in the big picture of God's plan.
Bill Hybels

Fighting Panic

Anxiety in the heart of man causes depression,
but a good word makes it glad.

PROVERBS 12:25 NKJV

We live in an uncertain world, a world that sometimes feels like shifting sand beneath our feet. Ours is an anxious society in which the changes we face sometimes threaten to outpace our abilities to adjust. No wonder we occasionally find ourselves beset by feelings of worry and panic.

At times, our anxieties may stem from physical causes—chemical imbalances in the brain that result in severe emotional distress. In such cases, modern medicine offers hope to those who suffer. But sometimes our anxieties result from spiritual deficits, not physical ones. And when we're spiritually depleted, the best prescription is found deep inside the human heart. What we need is a higher daily dose of God's love, God's peace, God's assurance, and God's presence. And how do we acquire these blessings? Through prayer and meditation, worship, and faith in our Creator.

The thing that preserves a man from
panic is his relationship to God.
Oswald Chambers

Doing the Right Thing

*By this we know that we have come to know
Him, if we keep His commandments.*

1 JOHN 2:3 NASB

When we behave like thoughtful adults—and when we conduct ourselves in accordance with God's instructions—we'll be blessed in ways we cannot fully anticipate. When we seek righteousness in our own lives—and when we seek the companionship of those who do likewise—we'll reap the spiritual rewards God intends for us to enjoy.

Today, as you fulfill your responsibilities, hold fast to that which is good, and associate with folks who behave in like fashion. When you do, your good works will serve as a powerful example and as a worthy offering to your Creator. And you'll reap a surprising array of blessings as a result.

*If you want to be respected for your actions, then
your behavior must be above reproach.*
Rosa Parks

You Are Blessed

I will bless them and the places surrounding my hill. I will send down showers in season; there will be showers of blessing.

EZEKIEL 34:26 NIV

God has given us more blessings in our lives than we can count. But our greatest blessing—a gift that is ours for the asking—is God's gift of salvation through Christ Jesus.

Today, begin making a list of your blessings. You won't be able to make a comprehensive list, but take a few moments and jot down as many blessings as you can. Then give thanks to the Giver of all good things—God. His love for you is eternal, and His gifts are the best kind. And it's never too soon—or too late—to acknowledge those blessings.

God's kindness is not like the sunset—brilliant in its intensity, but dying every second. God's generosity keeps coming and coming and coming.
Bill Hybels

Joy 101

When a man is gloomy, everything seems to go wrong;
when he is cheerful, everything seems right!

PROVERBS 15:15 TLB

God promises that we can experience a special kind of abundance and joy. How can we claim these spiritual riches? By trusting God, by obeying His instructions, and by following in the footsteps of His Son, Jesus. When we do these things, God fills our hearts with His power and His love . . . and we experience a peace that surpasses human understanding.

Today, as you go out to meet the many obligations of life, remember to offer praise to your Creator and give thanks for His gifts. As a way of blessing your loved ones and yourself, be quick to share a smile, a kind word, or a hug. And be sure that you're always ready to share God's joy—and His message— with a world that needs both.

When I think of God, my heart is so full of joy
that the notes leap and dance as they leave my pen;
and since God has given me a cheerful heart,
I serve him with a cheerful spirit.

Franz Joseph Haydn

Healthy Habits

*Beloved, I pray that in all respects you may prosper
and be in good health, just as your soul prospers.*

3 JOHN 1:2 NASB

All habits begin as small, consistent decisions that may seem harmless and insignificant at first. But before long, habits gain the power to change, transform, and even define you. And you're not just forming habits for yourself; you're also helping to shape the habits of those around you. So it's always good to take an honest look at the habits that make up the fabric of your day.

Are you and your family members eating and exercising sensibly? Have you established healthy habits that will improve the chances that you and your loved ones will live long, healthy lives? Hopefully so.

Once you establish healthy habits, and when you reinforce those habits every day, you'll be surprised at how quickly your physical, mental, and spiritual health will begin to improve. So why not start forming those healthier habits today?

Begin to be now what you will be hereafter.
Saint Jerome

The Importance of Prayer

Rejoice evermore. Pray without ceasing. In every thing give thanks: for this is the will of God in Christ Jesus concerning you.

1 THESSALONIANS 5:16–18 KJV

In his first letter to the Thessalonians, Paul advised his friends to pray without ceasing. That advice is for us today, as well.

Prayer is a powerful tool for communicating with God; it's an opportunity to commune with our heavenly Father. Prayer is not a thing to be taken lightly or to be used infrequently. It is a force for improving our lives, for building our faith, and for improving our world.

Prayer shouldn't be reserved for mealtimes or bedtimes; it should be a steady presence and focus in our daily lives. So today, pray constantly. Talk to God about the big stuff and about the little stuff. He wants to hear from you. God is listening; when you pray, He will answer.

Nothing is clearer than that prayer has its only worth and significance in the great fact that God hears and answers prayer.
E. M. Bounds

The Morning Watch

*Every morning he wakes me. He teaches me to listen
like a student. The Lord God helps me learn.*

ISAIAH 50:4–5 NCV

Each new day is a gift from God, and if we're wise, we'll spend a few quiet moments each morning thanking the Giver.

Warren Wiersbe wrote, "Surrender your mind to the Lord at the beginning of each day." When you begin each day with your head bowed and your heart lifted, you'll be reminded of God's love, His protection, and His commandments. Then you can align your priorities for the coming day with the teachings in God's Word and the directions He has whispered to your heart.

If you haven't already done so, form the habit of spending quality time with your Father in heaven. You'll find it makes all the difference.

*Are you weak? Weary? Confused? Troubled? Pressured?
How is your relationship with God? Is it held in its
place of priority? I believe the greater the pressure,
the greater your need for time alone with Him.*

Kay Arthur

Your Source of Strength

Cast your burden upon the Lord and He will sustain you; He will never allow the righteous to be shaken.

PSALM 55:22 NASB

When you find yourself worried about the challenges of today or the uncertainties of tomorrow, ask yourself whether you're ready to place your concerns and your life in God's all-powerful, all-knowing, all-loving hands. If the answer to that question is yes, then you can draw strength today from the source of strength that never fails—your Father in heaven.

Even when trouble arrives at your door and threatens an extended stay, you can find comfort and courage in the certain knowledge that your Creator is keenly aware of your pain— and that He is willing and able to heal your broken heart.

So when tough times come, depend on God. He is trustworthy, now and forever.

Seeing that a Pilot steers the ship in which we sail, who will never allow us to perish even in the midst of shipwrecks, there is no reason why our minds should be overwhelmed with fear and overcome with weariness.

John Calvin

Choosing God's Value System

Choose my teachings instead of silver, and knowledge
rather than the finest gold. Wisdom is more precious
than rubies. Nothing you could want is equal to it.

PROVERBS 8:10–11 NCV

Whether you realize it or not, your life is shaped by your values. And the same goes for your family members. From the time you wake in the morning until the moment you lay your head on the pillow at night, your actions are guided by the values that you hold most dear.

Society seeks to impose its set of values upon you and your loved ones; however, these values are often contrary to God's Word (and thus contrary to your best interests). The world's promises are incomplete and deceptive; God's promises are unfailing. Your challenge is to build your value system upon the firm foundation of God's promises.

Character is what a man is in the dark.
D. L. Moody

Passing Through the Storms of Life

*Jesus responded, "Why are you afraid? You have so
little faith!" Then he got up and rebuked the wind
and waves, and suddenly there was a great calm.*

MATTHEW 8:26 NLT

Sometimes, like Jesus's disciples, we feel threatened by the storms of life. During these moments, when our hearts are flooded with uncertainty, we must remember that God is not far off: He's right here with us.

Have you ever felt your faith in God slipping away? Even the most faithful Christians are, at times, beset by occasional bouts of discouragement and doubt. But even when you feel far removed from God, He never leaves your side. He is always with you, always strong enough to calm your life's storms—and even use them for your good. When you sincerely seek His presence—and when you genuinely endeavor to establish a deeper, more meaningful relationship with God—He will calm your fears, answer your prayers, and restore your soul.

God will make obstacles serve His purpose.
Lettie B. Cowman

The Courage to Believe

It is pleasant to see dreams come true, but fools refuse to turn from evil to attain them.

PROVERBS 13:19 NLT

It takes courage to dream big dreams. You will discover that courage when you do three things: accept the past, trust God to handle the future, and make the most of the time He has given you today.

How big are you willing to dream? Do you believe that God can perform miracles in your own life and in the lives of your loved ones? Are you willing to ask Him to move mountains in your life? Are you willing to do the work He requires? Hopefully so. After all, no dreams are too big for God.

So don't lose another day, another hour, or another minute. Start dreaming big dreams today. Then start working—and praying—to make those dreams come true.

If one advances confidently in the direction of his dreams, and endeavors to live the life he has imagined, he will meet with success unexpected in common hours.
Henry David Thoreau

Sharing Words of Hope

*Let's see how inventive we can be in encouraging
love and helping out, not avoiding worshiping
together as some do but spurring each other on.*

HEBREWS 10:24–25 MSG

Are you a hopeful, optimistic, encouraging person? And do you associate with like-minded people?

Hope cannot be constrained to just one person. When we surround ourselves with loving, positive people, they will lift us up. Right now, think of ways that you can encourage the people in your life—and ways that you can seek encouragement from others.

As a child of God, you have every reason to be hopeful—and you have every reason to share your hope with others. So today, look for reasons to celebrate and people to celebrate with. As you share hope, you'll build hope.

*We urgently need people who encourage
and inspire us to move toward God.*
Jim Cymbala

Serenity Now

The Lord says . . . "Do not think about the past. Look at the new thing I am going to do. It is already happening. Don't you see it? I will make a road in the desert and rivers in the dry land."

ISAIAH 43:18–19 NCV

Theologian Reinhold Niebuhr composed a profoundly simple verse known as the Serenity Prayer: "God grant me the serenity to accept the things I cannot change, the courage to change the things I can, and the wisdom to know the difference." Niebuhr's words are far easier to recite than to live by. Why? Because most of us want life to unfold in accordance with our own wishes and timetables. But sometimes God has other plans.

Today, ask God to give you the wisdom and courage to accept life as it comes. Trust Him to provide what you need, and you'll find real serenity.

Have courage for the great sorrows of life and patience for the small ones; and when you have laboriously accomplished your daily task, go to sleep in peace. God is awake.

Victor Hugo

Faith to Share

This and this only has been my appointed work: getting this news to those who have never heard of God, and explaining how it works by simple faith and plain truth.

1 TIMOTHY 2:7 MSG

Genuine faith was never meant to be locked up inside our hearts—to the contrary, it is meant to be shared with the world. Of course, if you wish to share your faith, you first must find it.

How can you find and strengthen your faith? Through praise, through worship, through fellowship, through Bible study, and through prayer. When you do these things, your faith will become stronger, and you'll find ways to share that faith with family members, with friends, and with the world.

So today, spend precious moments with your heavenly Father. And then share your faith and your enthusiasm with a world that needs both.

*Our faith becomes stronger as we express it;
a growing faith is a sharing faith.*
Billy Graham

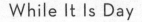

While It Is Day

*While it is daytime, we must continue doing the work of the
One who sent me. Night is coming, when no one can work.*

JOHN 9:4 NCV

John's words here remind us that "night is coming" for all
of us. But when we take God at His Word—and when we
take comfort in His promises—we need never fear the night.
After all, the Father has promised to love us and protect us.
Armed with these assurances, we can face life courageously,
seizing the opportunities He places before us each day.

Today is a priceless gift that has been given to you by
God—don't waste it. Don't stand on the sidelines as life's pa-
rade passes you by. Instead, search for the possibilities God has
placed along your path. This day is a one-of-a-kind treasure
that can be put to good use—or wasted. Your challenge is to
use this day joyfully and productively. And while you're at it,
encourage others to do likewise. After all, night is coming.

*The whole essence of the spiritual life consists in recognizing
the designs of God for us at the present moment.*
Jean Pierre de Caussade

Infinite Forgiveness

Forgive us our sins, for we also forgive
everyone who is indebted to us.

LUKE 11:4 NKJV

God's power to forgive is infinite—as is His love. Despite our shortcomings, despite our mistakes, God offers us immediate forgiveness when we ask Him. Despite our past failures, despite our weaknesses, God loves us still.

Because God has forgiven us—because He loves us in spite of our imperfections and frailties—we too should be quick to forgive others. As recipients of God's mercy, we should be merciful. When we offer forgiveness to others, God grants us the peace and contentment He wants us to know.

So when it comes to forgiveness, remember two simple truths: God offers His forgiveness to us; and we should offer our forgiveness to others.

It's as simple—and as wonderful—as that.

Forgiveness is the economy of the heart . . .
forgiveness saves the expense of anger,
the cost of hatred, the waste of spirits.
Hannah More

In His Hands

Don't brashly announce what you're going to do tomorrow;
you don't know the first thing about tomorrow.

PROVERBS 27:1 MSG

The world turns according to God's plans, not our wishes. No matter how carefully we plan, our plans may go amiss. So boasting about future events is best avoided, especially when we understand and acknowledge God's sovereignty over all things.

Are you planning and preparing for a better tomorrow? That's natural and even commendable; God rewards forethought just as He rebukes impulsiveness. The key is to submit all of our desires and plans to God's perfect will for our lives, knowing that He knows best.

So as you make your plans, do so with humility, consulting with and trusting in your heavenly Father. It's His hand that directs the future.

That we may not complain of what is, let us see God's hand in all events; and, that we may not be afraid of what shall be, let us see all events in God's hand.

Matthew Henry

His Rule, Your Rule

Here is a simple, rule-of-thumb guide for behavior:
Ask yourself what you want people to do for you,
then grab the initiative and do it for them. Add up
God's Law and Prophets and this is what you get.

MATTHEW 7:12 MSG

How do you treat your friends and family members? Is the Golden Rule your rule?

Jesus instructed us to treat other people in the same way we want to be treated. Yet sometimes, when we're feeling the pressures of everyday living, living by the Golden Rule can seem like an impossible task—but it's not.

Would you like to improve the quality of your life? Would you like to make the world a better place at the same time? If so, you can start by practicing God's Golden Rule. When you want to know how to treat other people, ask the person you see every time you look in the mirror. The answer you receive will tell you exactly what to do.

A man sins who wishes to receive more from his neighbor
than he is himself willing to give to the Lord God.
Saint Francis of Assisi

Your Way or God's Way

A man's heart plans his way, but the Lord directs his steps.
PROVERBS 16:9 NKJV

As you consider the path God wants you to follow, you will periodically ask yourself, "What now, Lord?" If you earnestly seek God's will for your life, you will find it . . . in time.

God never gives you an exact blueprint for your life. We don't know what will happen next. But we can keep praying and seeking God's heart, asking Him to move our hearts, inform our passions, and guide our paths. The more you do things His way, the more He'll reveal His way. Step by step, God will direct you . . . and there's no better way.

He watches over us in the storm, and He can bring us out of the storm when His purposes have been fulfilled.
Warren Wiersbe

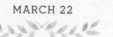

Ultimate Wisdom

Happy is the person who finds wisdom,
the one who gets understanding.

PROVERBS 3:13 NCV

When you find wisdom—and when you apply that wisdom to the challenges of everyday living—you'll enrich your own life and the lives of your loved ones. But the acquisition of wisdom is seldom easy or quick.

Do you seek wisdom? Then seek it every day of your life. Seek it with consistency and perseverance. And, most importantly, seek it in the right place. That place is, first and foremost, the Word of God.

If you study God's teachings, you will find the understanding you seek. And you'll find that no other source is adequate: God's wisdom is the ultimate wisdom.

Love Holy Scripture, and wisdom will love you. Love her,
and she will keep you. Honor her, and she will keep you.
Saint Jerome

The Right Kind of Habits

*Who among you is wise and understanding? Let him show
by his good behavior his deeds in the gentleness of wisdom.*

JAMES 3:13 NASB

If you sincerely desire to improve your spiritual health, you must honestly examine the habits that make up the fabric of your day. And you must abandon any habits that are displeasing to God.

If you trust your heavenly Father, and if you ask for His help, He can transform your life. If you sincerely seek Him, the same God who created the universe will help you defeat the harmful habits that have heretofore defeated you. So if at first you don't succeed, keep praying. God is listening, and He's ready to help you become a better person—the kind of person He created you to be.

*Habit is a cable; we weave a thread of it each
day, and at the last we cannot break it.*
Horace Mann

Never Lose Hope

*These things I have spoken to you, that in Me you
may have peace. In the world you will have tribulation;
but be of good cheer, I have overcome the world.*

JOHN 16:33 NKJV

There are few sadder sights on earth than the sight of a person who has lost all hope. But if you place your faith in God, you need never lose hope. After all, God is good; His love endures; He has promised us the gift of eternal life; and He always keeps His promises.

Consider the words of Jesus. He said, "I have overcome the world." Our world is indeed a place of trials and tribulations, but if we put our trust in God, we will be secure. God has promised us peace and joy. It's up to us to claim these gifts . . . and never lose hope.

*When you say a situation or a person is hopeless,
you are slamming the door in the face of God.*
Charles Allen

The Temptation to Judge

When they continued to ask Jesus their question,
he raised up and said, "Anyone here who has never
sinned can throw the first stone at her."

JOHN 8:7 NCV

As Jesus came upon a young woman who had been condemned by the religious leaders, He told the people gathered there that only the person who was without sin could cast the first stone. His message applied not only to those Pharisees of ancient times but also to us. If we genuinely want to experience God's peace and His joy, we must leave the judging to Him.

If you'd like to live a more peaceful, joyful existence, here's one important step you should take: resist the temptation to judge others. Don't gossip, don't denigrate, don't belittle, and don't malign. Instead, spend your time sharing God's love and spreading His message. After all, none of us is perfect. The world could use fewer judges and more witnesses: folks like you who are willing to share God's good news.

Forget the faults of others by remembering your own.
John Bunyan

Respecting Yourself

*To acquire wisdom is to love oneself; people
who cherish understanding will prosper.*

PROVERBS 19:8 NLT

Do you place a high value on your time and your talents? You should. After all, you were created by God with an array of unique gifts and opportunities, which He wants you to use effectively and efficiently. But if you've acquired the unfortunate habit of devaluing your efforts or yourself, it's time to revolutionize the way you think about your career, your capabilities, your opportunities, and your future.

Nobody can build up your self-confidence if you're unwilling to believe in your value as a child of God. And the world won't give you much respect until you show appropriate respect for yourself. So if you've been talking yourself down or selling yourself short, stop. Remember this: the God of the whole universe handcrafted you! You are precious in His sight.

*The first and worst of all frauds is to cheat
one's self. All sin is easy after that.*
Pearl Bailey

Calming Your Fears

Do not be afraid; only believe.

MARK 5:36 NKJV

Most of the things we worry about will never come to pass—yet we worry still. We worry about the future and the past; we worry about finances and relationships. As we survey the landscape of our lives, we observe all manner of molehills and imagine them to be mountains.

Are you concerned about the challenges looming ahead? If so, why not ask God to help you regain a clear perspective about the problems (and opportunities) that confront you? When you petition your heavenly Father sincerely and seek His guidance, He can touch your heart, clear your vision, renew your mind, and calm your fears.

Courage faces fear and thereby masters it.
Cowardice represses fear and is thereby mastered by it.
Martin Luther King Jr.

In Focus

Look straight ahead, and fix your eyes on what lies before you.
Mark out a straight path for your feet; stay on the safe path.
Don't get sidetracked; keep your feet from following evil.

PROVERBS 4:25–27 NLT

Every day is a chance to celebrate the life God has given you.
It's also a chance to give thanks to the One who has offered
you more blessings than you can possibly count. So what is your
focus today? Are you willing to turn your thoughts to God's
blessings and embrace His promises? Or will you focus your
energies on other things?

Today, why not fix your eyes on the comfort and joy that
can be yours? Why not take time to celebrate God's glorious
creation? Why not entrust all your hopes and fears to your
heavenly Father? When you do, you'll be able to think more
optimistically and faithfully about yourself and your world . . .
and then you can share your faith-based optimism with others.
They'll be better for it, and so will you.

*The greatest honor we can give Almighty God
is to live gladly because of the knowledge of His love.*
Julian of Norwich

How to Recharge Your Batteries

Your Father knows what you need before you ask Him.
MATTHEW 6:8 NASB

Could you use a little extra energy? Or a lot? If so, you're not alone. All of us need to recharge our batteries from time to time. But here's a word of warning: if you need more energy, don't make a beeline for the medicine cabinet or the espresso bar, because you'll never find lasting strength in a pill bottle or a cup of java. If you're looking for strength that lasts, the best place to start is with God.

Are you (or someone you care about) living under a cloud of uncertainty? If so, ask God where He wants you to go, and then go there.

In all matters, ask for God's guidance, and avail yourself of His power. When you do, you can be certain that He hears your prayers . . . and you can be certain that He will answer.

When the dream of our heart is one that God has planted there, a strange happiness flows into us. At that moment, all of the spiritual resources of the universe are released to help us. Our praying is then at one with the will of God and becomes a channel for the Creator's purposes for us and our world.
Catherine Marshall

Using God's Gifts

Each of you should use whatever gift you have received to serve others, as faithful stewards of God's grace in its various forms.

1 Peter 4:10 tniv

Your Creator intends for you to use your talents. Will you honor Him by sharing these gifts with those around you?

If you're wise, you'll strive to make the most of your God-given talents—and while you're at it, you'll encourage your family and friends to do likewise.

Today, make this promise to yourself and to God: Vow to cultivate your gifts and use them to make your corner of the world a better place to live. It's the best way to show gratitude to God for the talents and opportunities He has entrusted to your care.

When God crowns your merits,
He is not crowning anything but His own gifts.
Saint Augustine

Getting to Know Him

Take up My yoke and learn from Me, because I am
gentle and humble in heart, and you will find rest for
yourselves. For My yoke is easy and My burden is light.

MATTHEW 11:29–30 HCSB

Oswald Chambers, author of the classic Christian devotional *My Utmost for His Highest*, advised: "Never support an experience which does not have God as its source, and faith in God as its result." These words serve as a powerful reminder that we are called to walk with God and to obey His commandments. God gave us those commandments for a reason: not to oppress us, but so that we might obey them and be blessed.

We live in a world that presents us with countless temptations to stray far from God's path. But if we're wise, we will defend ourselves against and resist these temptations. God has given us clear instructions for when we're confronted with sin: we should walk—or, better yet, run—in the opposite direction. The good news is, the better we know Him, the easier—and more comforting—that will be.

Bible history is filled with people who began the race
with great success but failed at the end
because they disregarded God's rules.
Warren Wiersbe

APRIL

God's Wisdom and Your Finances

*It is better to get wisdom than gold, and to
choose understanding rather than silver!*

PROVERBS 16:16 NCV

I f you've ever experienced money troubles, you know all about the sleepless nights that can accompany financial hardship. But the good news is this: your heavenly Father is ready, willing, and perfectly able to help you overcome every kind of problem, including the monetary kind.

Ours is a society in love with money and the things money can buy. But God cares about people, not possessions . . . and He cares about you. So study what God's Word has to say about discipline and about money. Pray about your resources. Ask the Creator for wisdom to spend wisely and strength to work diligently. Then do whatever it takes to live in accordance with *all* of God's teachings. When you do, you'll experience the peace—both financial and spiritual—that only God can provide.

*If a person gets his attitude toward money straight,
it will help straighten out almost every other area in his life.*
Billy Graham

An Offer of Peace

Peace I leave with you; My peace I give to you;
not as the world gives do I give to you. Do not let
your heart be troubled, nor let it be fearful.

JOHN 14:27 NASB

The beautiful words of John 14:27 remind us that God offers us peace—not the kind the world offers, but rather the kind as He alone can give. This peace is a precious gift from our Creator. All we have to do is to trust Him and accept that gift with praise on our lips and gratitude in our hearts.

Have you found the genuine serenity that can be yours through a relationship with God?

Today, open your heart to God's peace. It is offered freely; it has been paid for in full; it is yours for the asking.

Where the soul is full of peace and joy,
outward surroundings and circumstances
are of comparatively little account.
Hannah Whitall Smith

Lost in the Crowd

The fear of human opinion disables;
trusting in God protects you from that.

PROVERBS 29:25 MSG

Who will you try to please today: your God or your associates? Best-selling author and pastor Rick Warren observed, "Those who follow the crowd usually get lost in it." Instead of trusting God for guidance, we imitate our neighbors. And if we're not careful, we can place popularity above principles. Instead of seeking to please our Father in heaven, we strive to please our peers.

Our obligation is not to please or impress neighbors, friends, or even family members. Our obligation is to please an all-knowing, all-powerful God. When we do that and trust Him, we won't be crippled by fear of what others think.

Today and always, seek first to please your loving, heavenly Father. Then you'll never get lost in the crowd.

There is nothing that makes more cowards
and feeble men than public opinion.
Henry Ward Beecher

A Time to Rest

Truly my soul finds rest in God; my salvation comes
from him. Truly he is my rock and my salvation;
he is my fortress. I will never be shaken.

PSALM 62:1–2 NIV

Physical exhaustion is God's way of telling us to slow down. Yes, God expects us to work hard, but He also intends for us to rest. When we fail to take the rest we need, we don't live according to God's plan.

We live in a world that tempts us to stay up late. But too much late-night TV, combined with too little sleep, is a prescription for exhaustion.

If you're feeling completely and utterly drained—so exhausted that you can't keep up with everything—it's time to cast your anxieties, work, and obligations onto God. And getting some sleep won't hurt, either.

*Prescription for a happier and healthier life: resolve
to slow down your pace; learn to say no gracefully;
resist the temptation to chase after more pleasure,
more hobbies, and more social entanglements.*

James Dobson

The Shepherd's Gift

*My cup runs over. Surely goodness and mercy
shall follow me all the days of my life; and I will
dwell in the house of the Lord forever.*

Psalm 23:5–6 NKJV

Do you sincerely seek the spiritual riches the Creator offers
to those who give themselves to Him? Do you want to
enjoy the confidence and assurance that result from a genuine,
life-altering relationship with a loving Father? Then trust Him
completely, and follow Him without reservation. When you
do, you will receive the love and abundance He has promised.

Today, and every day hereafter, open your heart to God.
Let Him fill it with the joy, the comfort, and the blessings the
Shepherd offers His sheep.

*God cannot give us a happiness and peace apart from
Himself, because it is not there. There is no such thing.*
C. S. Lewis

Face-to-Face with Old Man Trouble

When you go through deep waters, I will be with
you. When you go through rivers of difficulty, you
will not drown. When you walk through the fire of
oppression, you will not be burned up; the flames will
not consume you. For I am the Lord, your God.

ISAIAH 43:2–3 NLT

All of us encounter occasional setbacks—those inevitable
visits from Old Man Trouble. The fact that we encounter
adversity is not nearly as important as the way we choose to
deal with it.

When tough times arrive, we have to make a choice: we
can choose to begin the difficult work of tackling our troubles . . . or we can choose to cower in the corner. When we
summon the courage to look Old Man Trouble squarely in the
eye, more often than not, he blinks . . . and sometimes he even
retreats. God, on the other hand, never leaves us—not even
for a moment. God's love never falters, and it never fails and
because God remains steadfast, we have great comfort even in
the midst of trouble and we can live courageously.

*The closer we are to the Shepard, the
safer we are from the wolves.*
C. H. Spurgeon

Full Confidence

May the God of hope fill you with all joy and
peace as you trust in Him, so that you may overflow
with hope by the power of the Holy Spirit.

ROMANS 15:13 NIV

A re you confident, or do you live under a cloud of uncertainty and doubt? The answer to this question will determine, in large part, how you view your family, your future, your work, and your world. As the saying goes, "Attitude determines altitude." The higher your hopes, the higher you're likely to soar.

Yet even the most confident person will encounter situations that raise doubts and fears. When you see those inevitable storm clouds on the horizon, don't ever lose hope. After all, you're part of a loving family, you possess unique talents, you have the determination and the courage to tackle your problems, and you are always in the presence of the Ultimate Partner. With God by your side, you have every reason to be confident.

Oh, how great peace and quietness would he possess
who should cut off all vain anxiety and
place all his confidence in God.
Thomas à Kempis

Belief and Behavior

If we live in the Spirit, let us also walk in the Spirit.

GALATIANS 5:25 NKJV

It's never enough for us to simply hear God's instructions; we must also live by them. Do you believe the words of God? Does your behavior match your beliefs?

Today, make every encounter an opportunity to serve; make every word an effort to encourage family, friends, and even strangers.

Don't be afraid to stand up for your beliefs. Remember this: in the battle of vice versus virtue, the opposition never takes a day off . . . but neither does God. He'll comfort and strengthen you to live out His instructions for a faithful life.

We must, without apology, without fear, without ceasing, preach and practice our beliefs, carrying them out to the point of suffering.

R. G. Lee

Taking Care of Your Temple

Don't you know that you are God's temple
and that God's Spirit lives in you?

1 CORINTHIANS 3:16 NCV

God has a plan for every aspect of our lives, and His plan includes provisions for our physical well-being. But He expects us to do our fair share of the work! We live in a world in which leisure is glorified and consumption is commercialized. But God has better plans for His children. He does not intend for us to take our health for granted. To the contrary, He wants us to treat our bodies like temples . . . because that's precisely what they are.

In a world that is chock-full of tasty temptations, it's all too easy to make unhealthy choices. Our challenge is to resist those unhealthy temptations. Self-discipline is one means of doing that, but so is prayer. Today, ask your Creator to help you take care of the body He so carefully and wonderfully created. When you ask for God's help, He will give it—and you'll feel better inside and out.

Take care of your body.
It's the only place you have to live.
Jim Rohn

Character Counts

Lead a quiet and peaceable life in all godliness and honesty.
1 TIMOTHY 2:2 KJV

When we seek to live each day with discipline, honesty, and faith, at least two things happen: integrity becomes a habit, and God blesses us because of our obedience to Him.

Living a life of integrity isn't always the easiest way, but it is always the right way . . . and God clearly intends that it should be our way.

Character is built slowly over a lifetime and is a precious thing—difficult to develop, wonderful to witness. As thoughtful adults, we must seek to live each day with discipline, honesty, and faith. When we do, integrity becomes a habit. And God smiles.

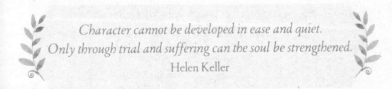

Character cannot be developed in ease and quiet.
Only through trial and suffering can the soul be strengthened.
Helen Keller

Choosing Wisely

The wisdom that is from above is first pure, then peaceable, gentle, willing to yield, full of mercy and good fruits, without partiality and without hypocrisy.

JAMES 3:17 NKJV

Because we possess free will, we make choices—lots of them. When we make choices that are pleasing to our heavenly Father, we are blessed. When we make choices that keep us following in the footsteps of God's Son, we enjoy the abundance Jesus promised to those who follow Him. But when we make choices that are displeasing to God, we sow seeds that have the potential to bring forth an unhappy harvest.

Today, as you encounter the challenges of everyday living, you will make hundreds of choices. Choose wisely. Remember that every choice that is displeasing to God is the wrong choice—no exceptions. So make your thoughts and your actions pleasing to God. Then you'll know the deep comforts of His pleasure and peace.

We are either the masters or the victims of our attitudes. It is a matter of personal choice. Who we are today is the result of choices we made yesterday. Tomorrow, we will become what we choose today.

John Maxwell

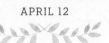

The Greatest of These

These three remain: faith, hope and love.
But the greatest of these is love.

1 CORINTHIANS 13:13 NIV

The familiar words of 1 Corinthians 13 remind us of the importance of love. Faith is vital, of course. So, too, is hope. But love is more important still.

Jesus showed His love for us on the cross, and we are called upon to return His love by sharing it. We are to love one another just as Christ loved us (John 13:34). That's a tall order, but we must follow it.

Sometimes love is easy (puppies and sleeping children come to mind), and sometimes love is hard (fallible human beings come to mind). But God's Word is clear: we are to love all our friends and neighbors, not just the "lovable" ones. So today, take time to spread God's message—and His love—by word and by example. It's not easy, but it's the greatest thing you can do.

The cross symbolizes a cosmic as well as a historic truth.
Love conquers the world, but its victory is not an easy one.
Reinhold Niebuhr

Need Directions?

*Man does not live on bread alone, but on every
word that comes from the mouth of God.*

MATTHEW 4:4 NIV

As you look to the future and decide upon the direction of
your life, what will you use as your road map? Will you
trust God's Word and use it as an indispensable tool to guide
your steps? Or will you choose a different map to plot your
course? The map you choose will determine the quality of your
journey and its ultimate destination.

So today consult God's instruction book with an open
mind and a prayerful heart. When you do, you can take comfort in the knowledge that you are being guided by a source of
wisdom that never fails.

*I believe the Bible is the best gift
God has ever given to man.*
Abraham Lincoln

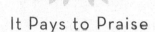

It Pays to Praise

*Through Jesus let us always offer to God our sacrifice
of praise, coming from lips that speak his name.*

<small>HEBREWS 13:15 NCV</small>

The Bible makes it clear: it pays to praise God. But sometimes we allow ourselves to become so preoccupied with the demands of everyday life that we forget to say thank you to the Giver of all good gifts.

Worship and praise should be a part of everything we do. Otherwise, we quickly lose perspective as we fall prey to the demands of the moment.

Do you sincerely desire to be a worthy servant of the One who has given you eternal love and eternal life? Of course you do! So praise Him for who He is and for what He has done for you. And one more thing: don't just praise Him on Sunday morning. Praise Him all day long, every day, for as long as you live . . . and then for all eternity.

*Two wings are necessary to lift our souls toward God:
prayer and praise. Prayer asks. Praise accepts the answer.*

Lettie Cowman

During Difficult Days

It will be hard when all these things happen to you.
But after that you will come back to the Lord your
God and obey him, because the Lord your God is a
merciful God. He will not leave you or destroy you.

DEUTERONOMY 4:30–31 NCV

All of us face difficult days. Sometimes even the most saintly men and women can become discouraged, and you are no exception. Hard times visit everyone, so you should prepare yourself and your loved ones for life's inevitable darker days. What's required is a combination of faith, work, wisdom, courage, and teamwork. When you stand united with friends and family in the face of adversity, no problem is too big for you to tackle.

If you find yourself in difficult circumstances, remember that God is merciful and faithful. If you become discouraged with the direction of your day, or your life, lift your thoughts and prayers to Him. He will comfort you and guide you through your difficulties . . . and beyond them.

*When life is difficult, God wants us to
have a faith that trusts and waits.*
Kay Arthur

Expressing Your Emotions

There is a time for everything . . . a time to weep and a time to laugh, a time to mourn and a time to dance.

ECCLESIASTES 3:1, 4 NIV

God gave us emotions, and He intends for us to express them. When we express our emotions sincerely, we can bring joy or even begin the process of healing. But if we suppress our emotions, or if we ignore our feelings altogether, we may needlessly prolong our pain.

If you've experienced a significant loss or a profound disappointment, don't bottle up everything inside. Express your feelings; talk openly to loved ones; allow tears to flow. Even if you'd rather ignore your pain, don't do it. Reach out to the people you love and trust.

By honestly expressing your grief, you will take an active role in God's plan for your recovery. And in time, you'll experience the comfort and the joy that can be yours—and that God wants you to know.

Christians are told not to stifle their grief or to behave unscripturally stoic.
Charles Stanley

No Pity Parties

The nights of crying your eyes out give way to days of laughter.
PSALM 30:5 MSG

Self-pity is not only an unproductive way to think, it's also an affront to our Father in heaven. God's Word promises that His children can receive peace, comfort, love, and eternal life. These gifts are an outpouring from God, a manifestation of His grace. With these rich blessings, how can we possibly feel sorry for ourselves?

Self-pity and peace cannot coexist in the same mind. Bitterness and joy cannot coexist in the same heart. Thanksgiving and despair are mutually exclusive. So if you're allowing thoughts of pain and worry to dominate your life, train yourself to think less about your troubles and more about God's blessings. Hasn't He given you enough blessings to occupy your thoughts all day, every day, from now on? So focus your mind on Him, and skip the pity party. You have better things to do!

A complete holiday from self-pity is necessary to success.
Dorothea Brande

Friendships That Honor God

Blessed is the man who walks not in the counsel of the ungodly, nor stands in the path of sinners, nor sits in the seat of the scornful; but his delight is in the law of the Lord, and in His law he meditates day and night.

PSALM 1:1–2 NKJV

B ecause we tend to become like our friends, we must choose those friends carefully. Some friends encourage us to work hard, to behave rationally, to do the right thing, and to honor God. These friendships should be nurtured. Other friends may place us in situations where we're likely to get into trouble— that kind of friendship has the potential to do us great harm.

Since our friends influence us in ways that are both subtle and powerful, we must ensure that our friendships are pleasing to God. When we spend our days in the presence of spiritually minded and clearheaded comrades, we'll be comforted and blessed—not only by those friends, but also by our Creator.

I have found that the closer I am to the godly people around me, the easier it is for me to live a righteous life because they hold me accountable.
John MacArthur

Faith and Family

The fundamental fact of existence is that this trust
in God, this faith, is the firm foundation under
everything that makes life worth living.

HEBREWS 11:1 MSG

Would you like to strengthen the ties that bind your family together? Here's a wonderful place to start: by strengthening your faith in God.

Every family is a series of successes and failures, celebrations and disappointments, joys and sorrows. Every step of the way, through every triumph and tragedy, God will stand by you and strengthen you. Your job is to let Him do precisely that.

When you and your loved ones place your faith, your trust, indeed your lives in the hands of the Creator, you'll be amazed at the marvelous things He can do with you and through you. So strengthen your faith and your family through praise, through worship, through Bible study, and through prayer. And trust God's plans. He will never let you down.

Faith is not a feeling; it is action. It is a willed choice.
Elisabeth Elliot

Expecting the Best

We are saved by hope.

ROMANS 8:24 KJV

D o you believe that God has wonderful things in store for you and your loved ones? As you plan for the next stage of your life's journey, promise yourself that when it comes to the truly important things in life, you won't settle for second best. What are the "important things"? Your faith and your relationships, for starters. In each of these areas, determine to be a rip-roaring, top-drawer success.

If you've entrusted your life to God, you have every reason to be hopeful. And if you remain faithful to His teachings and open to His love, you can expect to receive His richest blessings. So set God-centered goals (prayerfully), work hard (faithfully), and dare to dream (confidently). When you do, you can expect, through faith, to receive God's best gifts.

Hope is nothing else than the expectation of those things which faith has believed to have been truly promised by God.

John Calvin

Saying Yes to God

Fear not, for I am with you.

ISAIAH 41:10 NKJV

Your decision to seek a deeper relationship with God won't remove all problems from your life; to the contrary, it may bring about a series of personal crises as you constantly seek to say yes to God when the world pressures you to do otherwise. Each time you are tempted to distance yourself from the Creator, you face a spiritual crisis. A few of these crises may be monumental in scope, but most will be the small, everyday decisions of life. In fact, life can be seen as one test after another—and with each crisis comes yet another opportunity to grow closer to God, or to distance yourself from His plan for your life.

Today you will face many opportunities to say yes to God—and you will encounter many opportunities to say no to Him. Your answers will determine not only the quality of your day, but also the direction of your life. Step out in faith, and just say yes!

God provides for those who trust.
George Herbert

Making Difficulties Disappear

We also rejoice in our afflictions, because we know that affliction produces endurance, endurance produces proven character, and proven character produces hope.

ROMANS 5:3–4 HCSB

J ohn Quincy Adams observed, "Courage and perseverance have a magical talisman, before which difficulties disappear and obstacles vanish into air." When we attack our problems courageously—and keep attacking them—the result of our endurance will often bring success. But we know it's a matter of perseverance, not prestidigitation.

Do you seek a "magic talisman" that will help ensure that you receive the rewards you desire from life? No need to look in the local magic shop; instead, look to God and ask Him to give you strength to keep working even when you'd rather quit. Find the courage to stand firm in the face of adversity.

Press on. Obstacles are seldom the same size tomorrow as they are today.
Robert Schuller

His Rightful Place

You shall have no other gods before Me.

EXODUS 20:3 NKJV

A relationship with God sometimes seems far away from us; we can't call Him on the phone, or physically go to His house. Because of this, it's easy to put God on the back burner of our lives, and only reach out in prayer when we need something from Him. But this isn't the way it should be.

Are you willing to place God first in your life? Are you willing to welcome Him into your heart? Unless you can honestly answer these questions with a resounding yes, your relationship with God isn't what it could be or should be. But God is always available, and He's always ready to forgive. He offers greater comfort and blessing than you'll find anywhere else. Your heavenly Father loves you and wants a close relationship with you, not a distant one. He's waiting to hear from you now. Will you call on Him?

When you use your life for God's glory,
everything you do can become an act of worship.
Rick Warren

Take Time to Be Kind

As those who have been chosen of God, holy
and beloved, put on a heart of compassion,
kindness, humility, gentleness and patience.

COLOSSIANS 3:12 NASB

The instructions of Colossians 3:12 are unambiguous: we are to be compassionate, humble, gentle, and kind. But sometimes, when the pressures of daily life weigh heavily upon our shoulders, we fall short. Amid the busyness and confusion of our everyday responsibilities, we may neglect to share a kind word or a kind deed. This oversight hurts others, yes, but perhaps it hurts us most of all.

Today, slow down enough to be alert to those who need comforting words, a helping hand, or a heartfelt hug. Make kindness a hallmark of your dealings with others. They will be blessed, you will be blessed, and God will be honored.

*Kind words can be short and easy to speak,
but their echoes are truly endless.*
Mother Teresa

Working to Become the Best You

First plant your fields; then build your barn.

PROVERBS 24:27 MSG

How do you define success? Do you define it as the accumulation of material possessions or the adulation of your neighbors? If so, you need to rethink your priorities. Genuine success has little to do with fame or fortune; it has everything to do with God's gift of love and His promise of spiritual abundance.

Success in God's eyes lies in the ability to place more importance on doing the work He has set before you than on striving for recognition. So if you want to be a true success, forget about being successful. Concentrate, instead, on honoring God by doing your best and becoming the best "you" you can be. Your Creator has bestowed you with gifts—and he wants you to use them.

The great law of culture: Let each become all that he was created capable of being.
Thomas Carlyle

New Beginnings

I will give you a new heart and put a new spirit in you.

EZEKIEL 36:26 NIV

Life is constantly changing. Our circumstances change; our opportunities change; our responsibilities change; and our relationships change. Sometimes, when we reach the crossroads of life, we may feel the need for a jump-start—or the need to start over from scratch.

Are you in search of a new beginning? If so, don't be fooled into thinking that new circumstances will suddenly transform you into the person you want to become. If you feel the need for a fresh start, talk to God today. He specializes in new beginnings—starting in your own heart.

Receive every day as a resurrection from death, as a new enjoyment of life, meet every rising sun with such sentiments of God's goodness, as if you had seen it, and all things new—created upon your account.
William Law

Keeping Up with the Joneses

A pretentious, showy life is an empty life;
a plain and simple life is a full life.

PROVERBS 13:7 MSG

As a member of this highly competitive, twenty-first-century world, you know that the demands and expectations of everyday living can seem overwhelming at times. Keeping up with the Joneses can become a full-time job. A better strategy is to stop trying to please the neighbors and to concentrate on pleasing God.

Perhaps you've set your goals high; if so, congratulations! You're willing to dream big dreams, and that's a good thing. But as you consider your life's purpose, don't allow your quest for excellence to interfere with the spiritual journey God has planned for you. Strive to please God first and always. How? By welcoming Him into your heart and by following His lead. All other concerns will fall into proper perspective when we keep our eyes on God.

Ambition! We must be careful what we mean by it. If it means the desire to get ahead of other people—which is what I think it does mean—then it is bad. If it means simply wanting to do a thing well, then it is good.

C. S. Lewis

Make Prayer a Habit

Let everyone who is godly pray to You.

PSALM 32:6 NASB

If we are to maintain righteous minds and compassionate hearts, we must take time each day for prayer and meditation. We must make ourselves still in the presence of our Creator. We must quiet our minds and our hearts so that we might sense God's will and His love.

Prayer is a powerful tool for spiritual growth and a powerful tool for changing your world. So here's a challenge: make prayer a habit. Begin early in the morning, even if you don't have a lot of time, and continue throughout the day. Remember, God does answer prayer; but He's not likely to grant requests you haven't made. Spend time with your heavenly Father today.

There are times when we simply don't feel like praying—and that is when we need to pray the most!
Warren Wiersbe

Mature Righteousness

Run away from infantile indulgence. Run after mature righteousness—faith, love, peace—joining those who are in honest and serious prayer before God.

2 TIMOTHY 2:22 MSG

An important part of growing up is learning the wisdom of doing what needs to be done when it needs to be done. The better part of maturity is understanding the value of doing the right thing . . . and that means living in accordance with God's instructions.

God's Word teaches us to be faithful, honest, generous, disciplined, loving, kind, humble, and grateful. When we act in these ways, we'll be rewarded with the comfort and peace God gives to those who trust Him completely and follow His path.

Would you like to experience this? Then don't look for shortcuts, and don't expect impulsivity or immaturity to bring happiness. Instead, determine to act and think like a mature, thoughtful, obedient adult. Then get ready to receive the rewards God bestows upon His children . . . who act like grown-ups.

All growth that is not toward God is growing toward decay.
George MacDonald

Give Me Patience, Lord, Right Now!

*We urge you, brethren, admonish the unruly, encourage
the fainthearted, help the weak, be patient with everyone.*

1 THESSALONIANS 5:14 NASB

He's known as the inventor of bifocals and the lightning rod, but one might also say that Benjamin Franklin was a coinventor of America. He was one of our nation's most vocal founding fathers, one of its most successful publishers, and one of its most creative scientists. Yet Franklin observed, "Genius is nothing more than a greater aptitude for patience."

Patience pays powerful dividends, especially when it means being patient with the folks you encounter in everyday life. So today, when you're tempted to respond angrily to the delays and inconveniences that befall us all, be a little kinder—and a little more patient—than you have been in the past. When you do, God will smile . . . and so will your friends and neighbors.

The greatest and sublimest power is often simple patience.
Horace Bushnell

MAY

Faith That Moves Mountains

If you have faith as a mustard seed, you will say to this mountain, "Move from here to there," and it will move; and nothing will be impossible for you.

MATTHEW 17:20 NKJV

A re you a mountain mover whose faith is evident for all to see? Do you trust God, and do you believe He will help you do big things for Him?

Because we live in a demanding world, all of us have mountains to climb and mountains to move. Moving those mountains requires faith, and plenty of it.

God needs more people who are willing to move mountains for His glory and for His kingdom. But the Almighty walks with you, ready and willing to strengthen you. Accept His strength today. On our own, we are small and limited; but by having faith in God, we can truly carry out the unbelievable for Him.

*Only God can move mountains,
but faith and prayer can move God.*
E. M. Bounds

Embracing God's Love

We know how much God loves us, and we have
put our trust in Him. God is love, and all who live
in love live in God, and God lives in them.

1 JOHN 4:16 NLT

Y ou know the profound love that you hold in your heart for
your own family or close friends. As a child of God, you
can only imagine the infinite love that your heavenly Father
holds for you.

God made you in His own image, and now, precisely
because you are a wondrous creation treasured by God, a question presents itself: What will you do in response to the
Creator's love? Will you ignore it or embrace it? Will you
return it or neglect it? That decision, of course, is yours and
yours alone. But make no mistake: when you embrace God's
love, you are forever changed. You feel differently about
yourself, your neighbors, your family, and your world.

Your heavenly Father—a God of infinite love and
mercy—is waiting to embrace you with open arms. Accept His
love today and forever.

*[God is] good and all-powerful, caring for each
one of us as though the only one in [His] care.*
Saint Augustine

Expect Success

May the Lord our God show us his approval and make our efforts successful. Yes, make our efforts successful!

PSALM 90:17 NLT

Neil Armstrong served as a U.S. Navy aviator in Korea and was a test pilot before he joined NASA as an astronaut. Then, as commander of *Apollo 11*, he took one small step that placed him forever in the history books as the first human to set foot on the moon. When questioned about his space flights, Neil Armstrong replied, "We planned for every negative contingency, but we expected success."

If you'd like to launch your life to new heights, take a hint from the first man on the moon: plan for the worst—but don't expect the worst. When it comes to your expectations, pray that your plans are in line with God's, have faith, and set your sights on success. Then, like Neil Armstrong, you can confidently shoot for the moon.

You live up—or down—to your expectations.
Lou Holtz

A Life of Fulfillment

You, O God, have tested us; You have refined us as silver is refined. . . . We went through fire and through water; but You brought us out to rich fulfillment.

PSALM 66:10, 12 NKJV

How can we find genuine fulfillment? Is it by trusting the world's promises or by achieving success as the world defines it? Hardly. Real fulfillment starts and ends with God, not with the world. When we trust God's promises, seek God's will, and live in accordance with God's teachings, we will experience the true fulfillment that only He can offer.

God's Word is clear: spiritual abundance is available to all who seek it. Count yourself among that number. Seek first a personal, transforming relationship with your Creator, and then claim the joy, the fulfillment, and the spiritual riches that can and should be yours.

I'm fulfilled in what I do.
I never thought that a lot of money or fine clothes—
the finer things of life—would make you happy.
My concept of happiness is to be filled in a spiritual sense.
Coretta Scott King

He Wants You to Serve

The greatest among you must be a servant. But those who exalt themselves will be humbled, and those who humble themselves will be exalted.

MATTHEW 23:11–12 NLT

As you seek to discover God's unfolding purpose for your life, you'll find yourself asking this question: How does God want me to serve my family and my community today?

Whatever your path, whatever your career, whatever your calling, you may be certain of this: service to others is an integral part of God's plan for your life.

Every single day of your life, including this one, God will give you opportunities to serve Him by serving His children. Welcome those opportunities with open arms. They are God's gift to you. And He will surely reward you for your willingness to share your talents and your time with the world.

Some people give time, some give money, some their skills and connections, some literally give their life's blood. But everyone has something to give.
Barbara Bush

Deciding to Do It God's Way

Teach me Your way, O Lord; I will walk in Your truth.

PSALM 86:11 NKJV

Each of us faces thousands of small choices each day, choices that make up the fabric of daily life. When we align those choices with the instructions in God's Word, and when we align our lives with God's will, we'll receive His peace, His joy, and His comfort. But when we struggle against God's will for our lives—when we insist on doing things our way and not God's way—we'll reap a less bountiful harvest.

Today you'll face thousands of small decisions; as you do, use God's Word as your guide. And while you're at it, pay careful attention to the still, small voice of God whispering in your heart. In matters great and small, seek the will of God and trust Him. He will never lead you astray.

In the center of a hurricane there is absolute quiet and peace. There is no safer place than in the center of the will of God.

Corrie ten Boom

How Much Does God Love You?

The Lord is good, and His love is eternal; His faithfulness endures through all generations.

PSALM 100:5 HCSB

How much does God love you? More than you can comprehend. God's love is as vast as it is timeless; it is a boundless love that defies human understanding. Yet even though you cannot fully understand God's love, you can respond to it.

Your loving heavenly Father never leaves you for an instant. In fact, He is with you right now, offering His protection and His strength. How will you respond to Him? Will you thank Him for His blessings, and will you praise Him for His gifts? I hope so. After all, the Creator deserves your thanks, and you deserve the experience of thanking Him.

So please don't wait until the fourth Thursday in November. Make every single day, including this one, a time of thanksgiving.

There is no pit so deep that God's love is not deeper still.
Corrie ten Boom

Wisdom and Perspective

Everyone who hears these words of mine and puts them into practice is like a wise man who built his house on the rock.

MATTHEW 7:24 NIV

S ometimes, amid the demands of daily life, it's easy to lose perspective. Life may feel out of balance, and the pressures of everyday living may seem overwhelming. What's needed is a fresh perspective, a restored sense of balance . . . and God's wisdom. If we call upon the Lord and seek to see the world through His eyes, He will give us guidance and perspective.

So choose God. When you trust His wisdom and accept His love, you'll regain your perspective . . . and so much more.

God's plan for our guidance is for us to grow gradually in wisdom before we get to the crossroads.
Bill Hybels

Love That Lasts

Above all, [put on] love—the perfect bond of unity.
COLOSSIANS 3:14 HCSB

Genuine love requires patience and perseverance. Sometimes we're sorely tempted to treat love as if it were a sprint. But genuine love is always a marathon, and those who expect it to be otherwise will be disappointed.

Building lasting relationships requires a steadfast determination to endure and a willingness to persevere, even when times are tough. To see the power of perseverance, we need look no further than the life of Jesus Christ. He finished what He began, and so can we.

So the next time you're tempted to give up on a relationship, take a moment to reflect on how Jesus would respond. He is always faithful, always loving toward you. Ask Him to fill your heart with His love so that you can bless others with a love that lasts.

I have found the paradox, that if you love until it hurts, there can be no more hurt, only more love.
Mother Teresa

Really Trusting God

*It is better to trust the Lord than to trust people. It
is better to trust the Lord than to trust princes.*

PSALM 118:8–9 NCV

Talking about trusting God is easy; actually trusting Him is
considerably harder. Genuine trust in God requires more
than words; it requires a willingness to follow God's lead, a willingness to accept His providence, and a willingness to obey His
commandments. These are not easy things to do.

Have you spent more time talking about Jesus than walking in His footsteps? If so, maybe it's time to have a little talk
with God. Thankfully, whenever you're willing to talk with
God, He's willing to listen. And the instant you decide to place
Him squarely in the center of your life, He will bless you with
his presence. A relationship with God is its own reward.

Do you seek a renewed sense of purpose for your life?
Then don't just talk about trusting God; trust Him completely.

*God is God. He knows what He is doing.
When you can't trace His hand, trust His heart.*
Max Lucado

Navigating Life's Changes

*The prudent see danger and take refuge, but
the simple keep going and suffer for it.*

PROVERBS 27:12 NIV

With each passing day, the pace of life seems to intensify, and everything that we held as constants—health, jobs, and even people—changes around us. Thankfully, God does not change. He is eternal, and so are the truths found in His Word.

Are you apprehensive about things in the future that you can neither see nor predict? If so, take comfort; you can place your faith, your trust, and your life in the hands of the One who does not change—your heavenly Father. He is the unmoving rock upon which you can build your life, this day and every day. When you do, you are secure.

When you come to a roadblock, take a detour.
Mary Kay Ash

The Simple Life

Whoever becomes simple and elemental again, like this child, will rank high in God's kingdom.

MATTHEW 18:4 MSG

In our world, it seems simplicity is in short supply. Think for a moment about the complexity of your daily life and compare it with the lives of your ancestors. Certainly you are the beneficiary of many technological innovations, but those innovations come at a price; our lives are busier and more cluttered with information than ever before.

Unless you take firm control of your time and your life, you may become overwhelmed by an ever-increasing tidal wave. It can even threaten your happiness. But your heavenly Father understands the joy of living simply, with the trust and joy of a child. He wants you to know this way of living. So do yourself a favor: keep your life as simple as possible. When you do, and when you return to childlike faith in your Father, you'll discover the joy and comfort of the simple life.

I believe that a simple and unassuming manner of life is best for everyone, best both for the body and the mind.
Albert Einstein

Rest and Health

Rest in God alone, my soul, for my hope comes from Him.
Psalm 62:5 hcsb

God promises that when we come to Him, He will give us rest—but we must do our part. We must take the necessary steps to ensure that we get sufficient rest and that we take care of our bodies in other ways, too.

Each of us bears a measure of responsibility for the general state of our own physical health. Certainly, various aspects of health are beyond our control: illness sometimes strikes even the most health-conscious men and women. But for many of us, physical fitness is a choice: it's the result of hundreds of small decisions that we make every day of our lives. If we make decisions that promote good health, our bodies respond. But if we fall into bad habits and undisciplined lifestyles, we suffer the consequences.

So today, treat your body as a priceless asset on loan from God. Take good care of yourself . . . you belong to Him.

You can't buy good health at the doctor's office—
you've got to earn it for yourself.
Marie T. Freeman

Confidence Restored

*I've told you all this so that trusting me, you will be
unshakable and assured, deeply at peace. In this godless
world you will continue to experience difficulties.
But take heart! I've conquered the world.*

JOHN 16:33 MSG

Are you confident about your future, or do you live under a cloud of uncertainty and doubt? If you trust God's promises, you have every reason to live boldly. Yet despite God's promises, and despite His blessings, you may, from time to time, find yourself tormented by doubts and negative emotions. When you do, step back and redirect your thoughts and your prayers.

Even the most optimistic men and women may be overcome by occasional bouts of fear and doubt. But even when you feel discouraged—or worse—remember that God is always faithful, and He is always with you. When you sincerely seek Him, He will comfort your heart, calm your fears, and restore your confidence.

*As I have grown in faith and confidence, I have known
more and more that my worth is based on the love of God.*
Leslie Williams

Give Thanks for Your Hard Work and Your Good Luck

Thanks be to God for His indescribable gift!
2 CORINTHIANS 9:15 NKJV

It's an old idea and a true one: "The harder you work, the luckier you are." You certainly know a few things about both sides of that equation—life is full of challenging moments and incredible blessings. The fact that you're still on the job fulfilling your role means you're probably working hard . . . and it also means you're incredibly fortunate.

Your life is full of unique blessings from the Creator, gifts that He expects you to cherish and care for. So, today, say a prayer of thanks. And as you think about your own personal mixture of hard work and good fortune, thank God for both.

Opportunities are usually described as hard work, so most people don't recognize them.
Ann Landers

It's a Matter of Discipline

*God hasn't invited us into a disorderly, unkempt
life but into something holy and beautiful—
as beautiful on the inside as the outside.*

1 THESSALONIANS 4:7 MSG

Christians who study the Bible are confronted again and
again with God's intention that His children (of all ages)
lead disciplined lives. God doesn't reward laziness or misbehavior. To the contrary, He expects His own to adopt a disciplined
approach to their lives. Yet we live in a world in which leisure
is often glorified and misbehavior is often glamorized. We inhabit a society where sloppy is in and neatness is out. We stand
by and watch as the media often puts bad behavior on a pedestal. But God has other plans.

God did not create us for lives of mischief or mediocrity;
He created us for far greater things. So wise disciples teach
discipline by word and by example, but not necessarily in that
order.

*Some people regard discipline as a chore.
For me, it is a kind of order that sets me free to fly.*
Julie Andrews

Modern-Day Discipleship

He has showed you, O man, what is good. And what does the Lord require of you? To act justly and to love mercy and to walk humbly with your God.

MICAH 6:8 NIV

When Jesus addressed His disciples, He warned that each one must "take up his cross and follow Me." In Jesus's day, prisoners were forced to carry their own crosses to the location where they would be crucified. Thus the message was clear: in order to follow Christ, the disciples must deny themselves and trust Him completely.

Nothing has changed since then.

If we sincerely want to be modern-day disciples of God's Son, then we must make Him the focus of our lives, not merely an afterthought.

Would you like to experience the peace, the joy, the comfort, and the contentment that come from being a disciple of the One from Galilee? Then find a way to pick up His cross and carry it. When you do, He will bless you . . . now and forever.

Discipleship is a decision to live by what I know about God, not by what I feel about him or myself or my neighbors.

Eugene Peterson

Laboring for the Harvest

I saw that the best thing people can do is to enjoy their
work, because that is all they have. No one can help
another person see what will happen in the future.

ECCLESIASTES 3:22 NCV

Once the season for planting is upon us, the right time to
plant seeds is when we *make* time to plant seeds. And
when it comes to planting God's seeds in the soil of eternity,
the only certain time that we have is now. Yet because we are
fallible human beings with limited vision and misplaced priorities, we may be tempted to delay.

If we hope to reap a bountiful harvest for God, we must
plant now by defeating a dreaded human frailty: the habit of
procrastination. Procrastination often results from our shortsighted attempts to postpone temporary discomfort.

A far better strategy is this: whatever "it" is, do it now.
When you do, you won't have to worry about "it" later.

*Rather than face the mere possibility of pain
we will not act at all . . . [or] do something
easier than we should attempt.*
Dorothea Brande

The Importance of Family

Love one another earnestly from a pure heart.

1 PETER 1:22 HCSB

God has blessed you with one of His most precious earthly possessions—your family and friends. In response to God's gift, be sure to treat your family with love, respect, courtesy, and care.

We live in a competitive world, a place where earning a living can be difficult and demanding. As pressures build, we may focus so intently upon our careers (or other obligations) that we lose sight, at least temporarily, of perhaps less urgent but more important needs. We must never overlook our families. As we establish priorities for our days and our lives, we'll be wise to place God first . . . and family next.

As the family goes, so goes the nation and so goes the whole world in which we live.

Pope John Paul II

Your Growing Faith

Let us stop going over the basic teachings about Christ again and again. Let us go on instead and become mature in our understanding.

HEBREWS 6:1 NLT

Building and sustaining our faith is an ongoing process—and requires ongoing work. But the work of nourishing our faith can and should be joyful. The hours we invest in Bible study, prayer, meditation, and worship can be times of enrichment and celebration.

As we build our lives upon the foundation of faith, we will discover that the journey toward spiritual maturity lasts a lifetime. But it is a journey rich with blessing.

Are you willing to spend time each day with God? Are you willing to study His Word and apply it to your life? Determine to do those things today (and every day), because as a child of God, you're never fully grown. You can continue "growing up" every day of your life. And that's exactly what God wants you to do.

God is teaching me to become more and more "teachable." To keep evolving. To keep taking the risk of learning something new . . . or unlearning something old and off base.

Beth Moore

God's Surprising Plans

*It is God who is at work in you, both to will
and to work for His good pleasure.*

<small>PHILIPPIANS 2:13 NASB</small>

Oswald Chambers's best-selling devotional book, *My Utmost for His Highest*, first saw print six years after his death in 1923. This devotional gem would never have been published had it not been for Gertrude Hobbs Chambers, who compiled the book from meticulous notes she had taken during her late husband's sermons and lectures.

In Jeremiah 29:11 God says, "I know what I am planning for you. . . . I will give you hope and a good future" (NCV). The story of Oswald Chambers teaches us that God can use us not just during our lifetimes; He may continue to use us long after we've gone on to our heavenly reward.

So today, trust God, get busy, and leave the rest to the heavenly Father whose plans for your life are far greater than you can imagine.

Never place a period where God has placed a comma.
Gracie Allen

First Things First

Pay careful attention, then, to how you walk.

EPHESIANS 5:15 HCSB

O n our daily to-do list, all items are not equal: certain tasks are extremely important, while others are not. So it's imperative that we prioritize our daily activities and give attention to each task in the approximate order of its importance.

The principle of doing first things first is simple in theory but more complicated in practice. Well-meaning family, friends, and coworkers have a way of making unexpected demands on our time. Add to that each day's share of minor emergencies; these trivial matters tend to draw our attention away from more important ones. On paper, prioritizing is simple, but to act upon those priorities in the real world requires maturity, patience, and determination.

If you don't prioritize your day, life will do the job for you. So your choice is simple: prioritize or be prioritized.

Things which matter most must never be at the mercy of things which matter least.
Goethe

God's Guidance and Your Path

Trust in the Lord with all your heart; do not depend on your own understanding. Seek his will in all you do, and he will show you which path to take.

PROVERBS 3:5–6 NLT

Proverbs 3:5–6 makes this promise: if you acknowledge God's sovereignty over every aspect of your life, He will guide your path. As you prayerfully consider the path God wants you to take, here are some other things you can do to keep on the right path: Study God's Word and be ever watchful for His signs. Associate with faith-filled, optimistic friends who will encourage your spiritual growth. Listen carefully to that still, small voice that speaks to you in the quiet moments of your daily devotional time. And be patient.

Your heavenly Father may not always reveal Himself as quickly as you'd like, but rest assured that He wants to use you in wonderful, unexpected ways. Your challenge is to watch, to listen, to learn, and to follow.

Only by walking with God can we hope to find the path that leads to life.
John Eldredge

Keep Possessions in Perspective

A man's life does not consist in the abundance of his possessions.

LUKE 12:15 NIV

All too often we focus our thoughts and energies on the accumulation of earthly treasures, leaving precious little time to accumulate the only treasures that really matter—the spiritual kind. Our material possessions have the potential to do great good depending upon how we use them. But if we allow the things we own to own us, we may pay dearly for our misplaced priorities.

Much of society focuses intently on material possessions; however, God's Word teaches us that money matters little when compared to the spiritual gifts the Creator offers to those who put Him first in their lives. So today, keep your possessions in perspective. Remember that God should come first and everything else next. When you give God His rightful place in your heart, you'll have a clearer vision of the things that really matter. Then you can joyfully thank your heavenly Father for the abundant spiritual blessings He sends your way.

True contentment comes from godliness in the heart, not from wealth in the hand.
Warren Wiersbe

He Renews Our Strength

Do you not know? Have you not heard? The Everlasting God, the Lord, the Creator of the ends of the earth does not become weary or tired. His understanding is inscrutable. He gives strength to the weary, and to him who lacks might He increases power.

ISAIAH 40:28–29 NASB

When we lift our hearts and prayers to God, He renews our strength. Are you almost too weary to lift your head? Then bow it. Offer your concerns and your fears to your Father in heaven. He is always at your side, offering you His love and His strength.

Are you troubled or anxious? Take your anxieties to God in prayer. Are you weak or worried? Delve deeply into God's Word. Bask in His presence in the quiet moments of your day.

Are you spiritually exhausted? Call upon your Creator to renew your spirit and your life. God will never let you down. He will always lift you up if you go to Him. When you ask for strength, He answers—so why not ask Him now?

Troubles we bear trustfully can bring us a fresh vision of God and a new outlook on life—an outlook of peace and hope.
Billy Graham

Leaving a Legacy of Wisdom

Choose my teachings instead of silver, and knowledge
rather than the finest gold. Wisdom is more precious
than rubies. Nothing you could want is equal to it.

PROVERBS 8:10—11 NCV

Whether it's your own kids, nieces or nephews, or mentees, what lessons are you teaching the children in your life?

Our greatest gifts to future generations are not denominated in dollars and cents, and our best bequests are not the material possessions we leave behind. Our greatest gifts are the timeless principles and enduring values we share (with our words) and demonstrate (with our deeds). So today and every day, think carefully about the things you stand for, and be sure to let others know precisely where you stand. When you do, you'll be leaving a lasting legacy to the children in your life, and to their children, and to generations yet unborn.

Children take more notice of what their parents do,
than what they say. Actions speak louder than words.
William Tiptaft

Giving It Your Best

*Even a child is known by his doings, whether his
work be pure, and whether it be right.*

PROVERBS 20:11 KJV

How does God intend for us to work? Does He intend for us to work diligently, or does He, instead, reward mediocrity? The answer is obvious. In God's eyes, hard work is rewarded. Yet sometimes we may seek ease over excellence, or we may be tempted to take shortcuts when God intends that we walk the straight and narrow path.

Today, give your best, and encourage your loved ones to do likewise. Wherever you find yourself, whether at home, at church, in the workplace, or just about anyplace in between, do your work, and do it with all your heart. God will bless your efforts and use you in ways that only He can understand. So do your job with focus and dedication. And leave the rest up to God.

*Excellence is not perfection, but essentially a desire
to be strong in the Lord and for the Lord.*
Cynthia Heald

Terminating the Tantrum

Bad temper is contagious—don't get infected.
PROVERBS 22:25 MSG

Temper tantrums are unproductive, unattractive, unforgettable, unnecessary, and uncomfortable. Perhaps that's why Proverbs 16:32 says, "Controlling your temper is better than capturing a city" (NCV).

If you've allowed anger to become a regular visitor at your house, ask God for wisdom, for patience, and for a heart that is so filled with love and forgiveness that it has no room for bitterness. Bitterness is emotional poison and crossness is corrosive. If you desire emotional peace and spiritual comfort, one important step is finding ways to control your temper.

God will help you terminate tantrums if you ask Him, so why not ask Him today? It'll be better than capturing a city—you may just recapture the goodwill and affection of those around you.

Keep cool; anger is not an argument.
Daniel Webster

The Direction of Your Thoughts

*My cup runs over. Surely goodness and mercy
shall follow me all the days of my life; and I will
dwell in the house of the Lord forever.*

PSALM 23:5–6 NKJV

God has given you not only the ability to think, but also the ability to control the direction of your thoughts. So how will you direct your thoughts today? Will you focus on your opportunities, your blessings, and your hopes for the future?

The quality of your thought life will help determine the quality of the rest of your life—so guard your thoughts accordingly. The next time you find yourself dwelling on something negative, refocus your attention on things positive. And the next time you're tempted to waste valuable time worrying or complaining, resist that temptation with all your might. Turn your thoughts to God and to the bountiful blessings of goodness and mercy He has bestowed on your life. You'll see that your cup's running over with good things.

*The life of strain is difficult. The life of inner peace,
being harmonious and without stress,
is the easiest type of existence.*
Norman Vincent Peale

Let's Laugh

Clap your hands, all you nations; shout to God with cries of joy.

PSALM 47:1 NIV

Life is serious business . . . up to a point. But no one's responsibilities should be so burdensome that you forgo your daily quota of chuckles, snickers, and guffaws. So please don't forget to laugh.

You don't have to be a stand-up comedian to see the humorous side of life, and you don't have to memorize a string of one-liners in order to enjoy good humor. Humor tends to come naturally when you enjoy healthy relationships. Plus, you're more likely to laugh if you don't take yourself too seriously.

So today, as you go about your daily activities, approach your relationships and your life with a smile on your lips and a chuckle in your heart. After all, God created laughter for a reason . . . and our Father indeed knows best. So laugh!

He who laughs lasts—he who doesn't, doesn't.
Author unknown

Making a Masterpiece

Give your entire attention to what God is doing right now, and don't get worked up about what may or may not happen tomorrow. God will help you deal with whatever hard things come up when the time comes.

MATTHEW 6:34 MSG

Coach John Wooden was inducted into the Basketball Hall of Fame twice—first as a player and then as a coach. As a player, he was a member of Purdue's 1932 national championship team. He then became a successful college coach. During his storied coaching career, he led UCLA to ten national championships, a record that remains unbroken. Coach Wooden's advice for life was straightforward: "Make each day your masterpiece."

Yesterday is in the past, and tomorrow is never guaranteed. That leaves one day—this one—in which you can create a work of art with your life. So follow the coach's advice and give this day the best you have to offer. When you do that, each day will become not just an individual masterpiece, but a part of the beautiful mosaic God is making of your life.

The past, the present, and the future are really one: they are today.
Harriet Beecher Stowe

JUNE

He Helps Us Endure

Patient endurance is what you need now,
so you will continue to do God's will. Then you
will receive all that he has promised.

HEBREWS 10:36 NLT

If you've led a perfect life with absolutely no foul-ups, blunders, mistakes, or flops. You can skip this day's devotional. But if you're like the rest of us, you know that occasional disappointments and failures are an inevitable part of life. Such setbacks are simply the price we must pay for growing and learning.

When we encounter the inevitable difficulties of life here on earth, God stands ready to protect us. God promises that He is never distant and that He is always prepared to guide us and protect us when we ask Him. And while we are waiting for God's plans to unfold, we can be comforted in the knowledge that our Creator can overcome any obstacle, even if we cannot.

*God does not promise to keep us out of the storms
and floods, but He does promise to sustain us in the storm,
and then bring us out in due time for His glory
when the storm has done its work.*
Warren Wiersbe

The Power of Words

Watch the way you talk. Let nothing foul or dirty come out of your mouth. Say only what helps, each word a gift.

EPHESIANS 4:29 MSG

The words we speak have the power to do great good or great harm. If we speak words of encouragement and hope, we can lift others up. When we do, the effect on us is uplifting, too.

Sometimes, when we already feel uplifted and secure, we find it easy to speak kind words. But other times, when we're discouraged or exhausted, we can scarcely summon the energy to pick up our own spirits, much less anyone else's. Yet God wants us to speak words of kindness, wisdom, and truth—no matter our circumstances, no matter our emotions. When we do, we share a priceless gift with the world, and we give glory to God.

Today, try to make your every word a gift. You'll discover that the joy of kindness is like honey: it's hard to spread it around without getting a little bit on yourself.

How many people stop because so few say, "Go!"?
Charles Swindoll

Are You Enthusiastic?

Those who hope in the Lord will renew their strength.
They will soar on wings like eagles; they will run and
not grow weary, they will walk and not be faint.

ISAIAH 40:31 NIV

A re you enthusiastic about your life and your faith? Are you genuinely excited about the upcoming day, the upcoming week, and the upcoming year? Are you optimistic about your life and your future?

If your zest for life has waned, now is the time to redirect your efforts and recharge your spiritual batteries. And that means taking a look at your priorities (to be sure you're putting God first) and counting your blessings (instead of your troubles).

Nothing is more important than your wholehearted commitment to your Creator. Faith should never be an afterthought; it should be your top priority, your most prized possession, and your deepest passion. When you become enthusiastic about your faith, you'll become enthusiastic about your life, too. And then you'll feel the renewed energy and strength only God can give.

Your enthusiasm will be infectious, stimulating,
and attractive to others. They will love you
for it. They will go for you and with you.
Norman Vincent Peale

Temporary Setbacks

No matter how many times you trip them up, God-loyal people don't stay down long; soon they're up on their feet, while the wicked end up flat on their faces.

PROVERBS 24:16 MSG

When we encounter the difficulties of life that are sure to come, God stands ready to help us. Our responsibility, of course, is to ask Him for help. When we call upon Him in heartfelt prayer, He will answer—in His own time and according to His own plan—and He will heal our hearts when we hurt. And while we're waiting for God's plans to unfold and for His healing touch to restore us, we can be comforted in the knowledge that our Creator can overcome any obstacle, even if we cannot.

As long as a person keeps his faith in God and in himself, nothing can permanently defeat him.
Wilferd Peterson

An Awesome God

The fear of the Lord is a fountain of life.

PROVERBS 14:27 NIV

God's hand shapes the universe—and it shapes our lives. The Creator maintains absolute sovereignty over His creation, and His power is beyond our comprehension. If we are wise, we'll develop a healthy respect for God and for His awesome power.

The Bible tells us that the fear of the Lord is the beginning of wisdom (Proverbs 1:7). But a healthy fear of the Lord also means the death of every other fear—because we sense and trust God's immense power to take care of us.

So today, as you face the sometimes scary realities of everyday life, instead of focusing on your fears, cultivate a reverent fear of God. Only then can your spiritual education—and your faith—be complete. Once you acknowledge God's power over everything, including you, you will have acquired the most important wisdom of all.

It is not possible that mortal men should be thoroughly conscious of the divine presence without being filled with awe.

C. H. Spurgeon

Recouping Your Losses

*Misfortune pursues the sinner, but prosperity
is the reward of the righteous.*

PROVERBS 13:21 NIV

H ave you ever committed a big-time blunder, a monumental mistake, or a super-sized slipup? Welcome to the club!
Everybody makes mistakes. That wasn't your first, and it won't
be your last.

When we take missteps in life, the best thing to do is to
correct them, learn from them, and pray for the wisdom not to
repeat them. When we take those positive steps, our mistakes
become lessons and our lives become adventures in growth, not
stagnation.

So here's today's big question: Have you used your mistakes as stumbling blocks or as stepping-stones? The way you
respond to those incidents will have a lot to do with how
quickly you regain your confidence . . . and how wisely you
plan your next stage of life's journey.

*You build on failure.
You use it as a stepping-stone.
Close the door on the past.*
Johnny Cash

Blessed by Worship

Happy are those who hear the joyful call to worship, for they will walk in the light of your presence, Lord.

PSALM 89:15 NLT

We should worship God in our hearts every day, but we should also worship in our churches, with fellow believers. When we do so, we'll discover the joys and the comfort that result from fellowship with friends and family members.

We live in a world that is teeming with temptations and distractions—a world where vice and virtue are locked in constant battle over our minds, our hearts, our souls, and our communities. But we play a part in the battle, too. We must try to avoid the pitfalls of modern-day life and focus, instead, on the unchanging principles of God's Word. One way we remain faithful to our Creator is through the practice of regular, purposeful worship—in our churches and at home. When we worship the Father faithfully and fervently, we will always be blessed.

Only participation in the full life of a local church builds spiritual muscle.
Rick Warren

God Can Handle It

*Do not be afraid or discouraged, for the Lord will
personally go ahead of you. He will be with you;
he will neither fail you nor abandon you.*

<small>DEUTERONOMY 31:8 NLT</small>

As children of God, we have every reason to live courageously. After all, God loves us and has promised to be
with us. But sometimes, because we are imperfect human beings who possess imperfect faith, we fall prey to fear and doubt.

The next time you find your courage stretched to the
limit, remember that your heavenly Father is as near as your
next breath. He is your shield and your strength; He is your
protector and your deliverer. Call upon Him in your hour of
need, and be comforted. Whatever your challenge, whatever
your trouble, God can handle it . . . and He will!

*Walk boldly and wisely in that light thou hast—
There is a hand above that will help thee on.*
Philip James Bailey

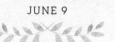

Actions Speak Louder

Be ye doers of the word, and not hearers
only, deceiving your own selves.

JAMES 1:22 KJV

Are you determined to make a difference in the lives of your family and friends? If so, you must make sure that your actions speak for themselves.

The old saying is both familiar and true: actions indeed speak louder than words. So it's up to you to make certain that your actions always speak well of your life and your legacy, backing up the beliefs that you espouse to those around you.

Sometimes you will be tempted to talk much and do little—you will be tempted to verbalize your beliefs rather than live by them. But it is never enough to wait idly by while others do the right thing; you, too, must act—starting now and ending never.

You may be disappointed if you fail,
but you are doomed if you don't try.
Beverly Sills

The Seeds of Happiness

*If they serve Him obediently, they will end their
days in prosperity and their years in happiness.*

JOB 36:11 HCSB

Before she became America's first First Lady, Martha Washington experienced the grief of losing her first husband. Yet despite the tragedies that she endured, Martha never allowed pessimism or doubt to cloud her vision. She said, "We carry the seeds of happiness with us wherever we go."

So the next time you're feeling troubled, fearful, apathetic, or blue, remember that wherever you go, you carry within you the potential to be happy. Realizing that potential is up to you, but it's always there.

*Many persons have a wrong idea of what constitutes
true happiness. It is not attained through self-gratification,
but through fidelity to a worthy purpose.*
Helen Keller

The Need for Self-Discipline

*Do you not know that those who run in a race all
run, but only one receives the prize? Run in such a
way that you may win. Everyone who competes in
the games exercises self-control in all things.*

1 CORINTHIANS 9:24–25 NASB

God's Word tells us clearly that we must exercise self-discipline in all matters. If we genuinely seek to be faithful stewards of our time, our talents, and our resources, we must adopt a disciplined approach to life. Otherwise, our talents will be wasted and our resources squandered.

The good news is, hard work and perseverance result in some of the greatest rewards we can experience. May we, as disciplined believers, be willing to work for the rewards—spiritual as well as material—we so earnestly desire.

*God provides the ingredients for our daily bread
but expects us to do the baking. With our own hands!*
Barbara Johnson

Always Forgiving

> Peter came to him and asked, "Lord, how often should
> I forgive someone who sins against me? Seven times?"
> "No, not seven times," Jesus replied, "but seventy times seven!"
>
> MATTHEW 18:21–22 NLT

How often should we forgive other people? More times than we can count. That's a tall order, but we must remember that it's an order from God. And even when God asks us to do something difficult, we can be assured that it's for our good—that He will help us to obey Him.

In God's curriculum, forgiveness isn't optional; it's a required course. That doesn't mean it's easy. Forgiving people who have hurt us deeply is one of the hardest things to do. But if we fail to forgive others, we hurt ourselves most of all. When our hearts are filled with bitterness, there's no room left for love.

Today, search your heart: note all the people you haven't yet forgiven . . . and forgive them. No matter how long you've held that grudge, it's never too late to let it go.

Having forgiven, I am liberated.
Father Lawrence Jenco

JUNE 13

Today's Journey

Be filled to the measure of all the fullness of
God . . . who is able to do immeasurably more
than all we ask or imagine, according to his
power that is at work within us.

EPHESIANS 3:19–20 NIV

This day, like every other, is full of opportunities, challenges, and choices. But no choice you make is more important than the choice you make concerning God. Today, you will either place Him at the center of your life . . . or not. And the consequences of that choice are both temporal and eternal.

Sometimes, without our even realizing, we gradually drift from the One we need most. Thankfully, God never drifts away from us. He remains always present, always steadfast, always loving.

As you begin this day, place God first in your thoughts, on your lips, and in your heart. And then, with the Creator of the universe as your guide and companion, you can face today's journey with courage.

*You cannot be the person God meant you to be,
and you cannot live the life He meant you to
live, unless you live from the heart.*
John Eldredge

Time for Silence

Be silent before Me.

Isaiah 41:1 hcsb

For busy people, each day can quickly be filled up with a wide assortment of responsibilities, distractions, interruptions, and commitments. And since you live in a modern and clamorous society, you're not exempt from the stress and the noise. Yet the noisier your world becomes, the more you need to carve out meaningful moments for silence and meditation.

God isn't a skywriter; He doesn't spread His instructions across the morning sky for all to see. To the contrary, God often speaks in a still, quiet voice, a voice that can be drowned out by the noise of the day.

So even if your calendar is filled from cover to cover, make time for silence. You should always have at least one serious chat with your Creator every day. He deserves it . . . and so do you.

Deepest communion with God is beyond words, on the other side of silence.
Madeleine L'Engle

Optimism Pays

*This hope we have as an anchor of the soul,
a hope both sure and steadfast.*

HEBREWS 6:19 NASB

In 1919, Conrad Hilton paid $5,000 for a small Texas hotel and began acquiring more properties. Over the years, his name became synonymous with quality and service. He even purchased New York's famed Waldorf-Astoria Hotel and made it the crown jewel in his chain. Hilton's advice for life was as expansive as Texas. He said, "Think big. Act big. Dream big."

If you've been plagued by pessimism and doubt, reconsider that way of thinking, and return to an attitude of faith and optimism. Good things do happen to good people, but the best things are usually reserved for those who expect the best and plan for it. So start dreaming in Technicolor. Think optimistically about your world and your life. Since dreams often do come true, you might as well make your dreams Texas-sized. There's no limit to what God can do!

*I am an optimist. It does not seem
too much use being anything else.*
Winston Churchill

Pleasing God

*Cheerfully pleasing God is the main thing, and that's
what we aim to do, regardless of our conditions.*

2 CORINTHIANS 5:9 MSG

When God made you, He equipped you with an array of talents and abilities that are uniquely yours. It's up to you to develop those talents and to use them, but sometimes the world will discourage you. At times, society will attempt to make you fit into a particular mold. Sometimes you may become so wrapped up in meeting those expectations that you fail to focus on God's expectations. But this is a mistake.

Whom will you try to please today, God or man? Your primary obligation is not to please imperfect people. Your obligation is to strive diligently to meet the expectations of an all-knowing and perfect God. Trust Him always. Love Him always. Praise Him always. And seek to please Him always.

*Don't be addicted to approval. Follow your heart.
Do what you believe God is telling you to do,
and stand firm in Him and Him alone.*
Joyce Meyer

Old-Fashioned Courtesy Still Matters

Be hospitable to one another without grumbling.

1 PETER 4:9 NKJV

Here in the twenty-first century, it sometimes seems like common courtesy is a decidedly uncommon trait. But if we are to trust the Bible—and we should—then we understand that our challenge is to make sure that kindness and courtesy never go out of style.

Today, make sure that you offer the gift of courtesy to family members, to friends, and even to total strangers. Be gentle, considerate, and well-mannered. And as you consider all the things that God has done for you, honor Him with your words and with your deeds. He expects no less; He deserves no less; and neither do the folks who cross your path.

Only the courteous can love,
but it is love that makes them courteous.
C. S. Lewis

A Storehouse of Knowledge

The wise store up knowledge.
PROVERBS 10:14 HCSB

I s your house a storehouse of both wisdom and knowledge? Knowledge can be found in textbooks or online; wisdom, on the other hand, is found in God's Holy Word and in the carefully chosen words of loving and thoughtful parents, friends, and mentors.

When we give others the gift of knowledge, we do them a wonderful service. Knowledge is an important building block in a well-lived life, and it pays rich dividends both personally and professionally. But wisdom is even more important, because it refashions not only the mind but also the heart. And when it comes to sharing the gift of wisdom, you have much to offer. So don't hesitate to share the lessons you've learned, even as you continue to learn from others.

*Let us remember that the longer we live,
the more we know, and the more we know,
the more beautiful we are.*
Marianne Williamson

The Answer to Adversity

God is our refuge and strength, a very present help in trouble.

PSALM 46:1 NKJV

From time to time, all of us must endure discouragement and defeat. We sometimes experience life-changing losses that leave us reeling. But when we do, God stands ready to help. When we are troubled, we can call upon God and in His perfect time and perfect way, He will heal us.

Are you anxious? Take those anxieties to God. Are you troubled? Take your troubles to Him. Does your world seem to be falling down around you? Seek protection from the One who cannot be moved. When you feel weak, give your troubles to God: He is strong. The same Being who created the universe will comfort and heal you—the answer to adversity is simply to ask.

When God is going to do a wonderful thing,
He begins with a difficulty. When He is going to do a
very wonderful thing, he begins with an impossibility.
Charles Inwood

Opportunities Abound

I can do everything through him who gives me strength.
PHILIPPIANS 4:13 NIV

Paradoxically, to make your dream come true, you have to stay awake and alert. That means keeping your eyes (and mind) open for new opportunities.

Whether you realize it or not, opportunities are whirling around you like stars crossing the night sky—beautiful to observe and too numerous to count. Yet we can get so preoccupied with the daily grind that we don't lift our eyes to the heavens to notice.

Today, take time to step back from the challenges of daily living. Lift your eyes toward heaven, and focus your thoughts on two things—on God and on the opportunities He has placed before you. If you let Him, He will lead you in the direction of those opportunities. So watch carefully, pray fervently, and then act accordingly.

With the right attitude and a willingness to pay the price, almost anyone can pursue nearly any opportunity and achieve it.
John Maxwell

Making the Most of Life

He who pursues righteousness and love
finds life, prosperity and honor.

PROVERBS 21:21 NIV

Of course, you've heard the saying "Life is what you make it." And although that statement may seem trite, it's also true. You can choose a life filled to the brim with frustration and fear, or you can choose a life of abundance and peace.

What's your attitude today? And what's the prevailing attitude of the people who live under your roof?

God created you in His own image, and He wants you to experience joy, contentment, peace, and abundance. And when is the best time to start reaping the rewards of positive thinking? Right now.

*It is God to whom and with whom we travel,
and while He is the End of our journey,
He is also at every stopping place.*
Elisabeth Elliot

A Fresh Start

Do not remember the former things, nor consider the things of old. Behold, I will do a new thing.

ISAIAH 43:18–19 NKJV

Each new day offers countless opportunities to celebrate life, to serve God, and to care for His children. But each day also offers opportunities to be hijacked by life's various complications and distractions. Thankfully, we are free to seek God's guidance whenever we choose. And whenever we ask Him to renew our strength and guide our steps, He will do so.

If you'd like to change some aspect of your life, consider this day a new beginning. Consider it a fresh start, a renewed opportunity to build a better life as you serve your Creator with willing hands and a loving heart. Ask God to renew your sense of purpose as He guides your steps. When you ask, He will answer.

This day is a glorious opportunity. Seize it while you can.

Every day we live is a priceless gift of God, loaded with possibilities to learn something new, to gain fresh insights.
Dale Evans Rogers

When Life Is Difficult

*Be strong and courageous. Do not be terrified;
do not be discouraged, for the Lord your God
will be with you wherever you go.*

JOSHUA 1:9 NIV

This world can be a daunting place, so even if you're the most faithful person in town, you may still find your courage tested by the inevitable disappointments and unspoken fears that accompany life here in the modern age.

The next time you find your courage tested to the limit, remember to take your fears to God. If you call upon Him, you will be comforted. Whatever your challenge, whatever your trouble, God can help you tackle it.

So don't spend too much time fretting over yesterday's failures or tomorrow's dangers. Focus, instead, on today's opportunities, and rest assured that God is big enough to meet every challenge you face . . . now and forever.

 *What is courage? It is the ability to be strong in trust,
in conviction, in obedience. To be courageous is to step
out in faith—to trust and obey, no matter what.*
Kay Arthur

Be a Worshipper

Worship the Lord your God, and serve only Him.

MATTHEW 4:10 HCSB

God has a wonderful plan for your life, and an important part of that plan includes worship. We should never deceive ourselves: every life is based upon some form of worship. The question is not whether we worship but what we worship.

Some of us choose to worship God. The result is a plentiful harvest of joy, peace, and comfort. Others distance themselves from God by worshipping earthly possessions and personal gratification. But that will yield only sorrow in the end.

Have you welcomed God into your heart? Then worship Him today and every day. Worship Him with sincerity and thanksgiving. Worship Him early and often. Worship Him with your thoughts, your actions, your prayers, and your praise.

It's the definition of worship: A hungry heart finding the Father's feast. A searching soul finding the Father's face. A wandering pilgrim spotting the Father's house. Finding God. Finding God seeking us. This is worship. This is a worshipper.

Max Lucado

Recognizing Your Blessings

Bless the Lord, O my soul, and forget not all his benefits.

PSALM 103:2 KJV

Howard Gerald "Jerry" Clower never told a joke you couldn't repeat in church, yet he sold millions of comedy records to adoring fans. Clower once said, "Lord, my cup runneth over and slosheth into the saucer."

Most of us are similar to Jerry: we have more blessings than we can count. But sometimes we forget to even try to count them.

Today, slow down and take inventory of the benefits you've received from your heavenly Father. And then add this to your list of blessings—the ability to recognize those blessings and to know the God who bestows them.

Don't have anything to be thankful for?
Check your pulse!
Church sign

When Times Are Stressful

I cried out to the Lord in my suffering, and he
heard me. He set me free from all my fears.

PSALM 34:6 NLT

Stressful days are an inevitable fact of modern life. And how
do we deal with the challenges of being a busy adult in a
demanding, twenty-first-century world? By turning our days
and our lives over to God.

Elisabeth Elliot writes, "If my life is surrendered to God,
all is well. Let me not grab it back, as though it were in peril in
His hand but would be safer in mine!" And her words ring true,
especially in these troubled times. When times are tough,
when daily stresses threaten to overwhelm us, God remains
steadfast, always ready to calm our fears and redirect our steps.

So the next time you feel stressed, call time out and call on
God. He's always with you, always loving, always ready to help.
And the rest, of course, is up to you.

*Don't be overwhelmed . . .
take it one day and one prayer at a time.*
Stormie Omartian

A God-Made Man

Respecting the Lord and not being proud will
bring you wealth, honor, and life.

PROVERBS 22:4 NCV

You've likely heard the phrase on countless occasions: "He's a self-made man." In truth, none of us is self-made. We all owe countless debts that we can never repay. Our first debt is to our Father in heaven—who has given us everything we are, everything we enjoy, and everything we ever will be—and to His Son, who sacrificed His own life on a cross so that we can be reconciled to God. We're also indebted to ancestors, parents, teachers, friends, spouses, family members, and coworkers . . . the list of those who've contributed to our lives in one way or another seems almost endless.

Most of us are happy to point to ourselves and take the credit for every positive accomplishment. But in our better moments, in the quiet moments when we search the depths of our own hearts, we know better. Whatever "it" is, God did that. And He deserves the credit.

Humility is not thinking less of yourself,
it's thinking of yourself less.
Rick Warren

Be Bold!

God doesn't want us to be shy with his gifts,
but bold and loving and sensible.

2 TIMOTHY 1:7 MSG

How does God intend for us to live? Does He want us to be timid and fearful, or does He intend for us to be confident and bold? The answer should be obvious. God offers us strength and the courage whenever we are wise enough to ask for them. Yet sometimes we may be tempted to take the easy way out even though God may be directing us toward a different, more difficult path.

Today, be bold in the service of your Creator, and encourage your loved ones to do likewise. Face your fears and do your best, knowing that with God on your side, you are protected. When you live courageously, God will bless your efforts and use you in ways that only He can understand.

Let us arm ourselves against our spiritual enemies
with courage. They think twice about
engaging with one who fights boldly.
Saint John Climacus

Media Messages and You

*To acquire wisdom is to love oneself; people
who cherish understanding will prosper.*

PROVERBS 19:8 NLT

Sometimes it's hard to have self-respect, especially if you pay much attention to all the messages that media and corporations keep pumping out. Those messages, which seem to pop up just about everywhere, try to tell you how you and your family should look, how you should behave, and what you should buy.

This kind of society isn't interested in making you feel better about yourself—far from it. It's interested in selling you products. And one of the best ways that marketers can find to sell you things is by making you feel dissatisfied with your current situation.

So don't fall prey to the media's messages about what you should buy and how you should change. You are wonderful just as you are . . . don't let anyone tell you otherwise.

*The world's sewage threatens to contaminate
the stream of Christian thought. . . . Is the
world shaping your mind, or is Christ?*
Billy Graham

Finding Encouragement

Be strong and courageous. Do not be terrified;
do not be discouraged, for the Lord your God
will be with you wherever you go.

JOSHUA 1:9 NIV

God offers us the strength to meet our challenges, and He offers us hope for the future. One way He communicates His message of hope is through the words of encouraging friends and family members.

Hope is something that must be nurtured if it is to grow.

Are you a hopeful, optimistic person who believes God has good plans for you? You can be assured that He does. Do you associate with those who understand God's loving nature? If so, you know just where to find encouragement—in your heavenly Father and with your spiritual brothers and sisters.

*Open your heart to sympathy,
but close it against despondency. The flower
which opens to receive the dew shuts against the rain.*
James H. Aughey

JULY

God's Big Plans for You

With God's power working in us, God can do much,
much more than anything we can ask or imagine.

EPHESIANS 3:20 NCV

Your heavenly Father wants only the best for you, and He can do wonderful things in and through you. Yet sometimes, especially if you've recently experienced a deep disappointment, you may find it difficult to envision a brighter future. If you're struggling in this way, perhaps it's time to take a second look at God's capabilities . . . and your God-given talents.

So even if you're going through difficult days now, don't abandon your dreams. Instead, trust that God is preparing you for greater things. His power is at work in you.

You cannot out-dream God.
John Eldredge

Success and Service

Prepare your minds for service and have self-control.

1 PETER 1:13 NCV

Young Amos Jacobs had given up on show business. But before quitting, he prayed a final prayer of desperation. The next day, he received a job offer that turned his career around. He changed his name to Danny Thomas, reinvigorated his showbiz career, and eventually became the beloved star of the popular TV sitcom *Make Room for Daddy.*

To give something back in gratitude for his blessings, Thomas endowed the St. Jude Children's Research Hospital in Memphis. He said, "Success has nothing to do with what you gain in life or accomplish for yourself. It's what you do for others."

If you desire to be a genuine success, make room to implement Danny's advice: find ways to give a little more than you get from life. If you do, your star, like Danny's, will keep shining today, tomorrow, and for generations to come.

You were created to add to life on earth, not just take from it.
Rick Warren

Aim at Heaven

Set your minds on what is above, not on what is on the earth.

COLOSSIANS 3:2 HCSB

If you wish to keep a comfortable conscience and a peaceful soul, you must distance yourself, at least somewhat, from the temptations and distractions around you. But distancing yourself isn't easy, especially when so many societal forces are struggling to get your attention, your participation, and your money.

C. S. Lewis advised, "Aim at heaven and you will get earth thrown in; aim at earth and you get neither." When you aim at heaven, you'll be strengthening your character as you improve every aspect of your life. And God will demonstrate His approval as He showers you with more spiritual blessings than you can count.

Whoever seeks earth before heaven will certainly lose earth as well.
Saint John Chrysostom

Comparison Kills

*Let us not become boastful, challenging
one another, envying one another.*

GALATIANS 5:26 NASB

In a competitive, cutthroat world, it is easy to become envious of others' success.

We know intuitively that envy is wrong, but because we are frail, imperfect human beings, we may find ourselves struggling with feelings of envy or resentment, or both. These feelings may be especially forceful when we see other people experience unusually good fortune. Comparison kills; not only does it damage our relationships with others, but it hurts our own hearts, too.

Have you recently felt the pangs of envy creeping into your heart? If so, it's time to focus on the marvelous things that God has done for you and your loved ones. And just as important, you must refrain from preoccupying yourself with the blessings that God has chosen to give others.

So here's a surefire formula for a happier, healthier life: count your own blessings, and let your neighbors counts theirs.

Discontent dries up the soul.
Elisabeth Elliot

When Things Aren't Perfect

May Your faithful love comfort me, as
You promised Your servant.

PSALM 119:76 HCSB

It's unavoidable: because you are an imperfect human being, you are not perfectly happy—and that's perfectly okay with God. He is far less concerned with your happiness than He is with your holiness.

God continuously reveals Himself in everyday life, but He does not do so in order to make you contented; He does so in order to lead you back to Him. So don't be overly concerned with your current level of happiness: it will change. Be more concerned with the current state of your relationship with the Creator: He does not change. And because your heavenly Father transcends time and space, you can be comforted in the knowledge that in the end His joy will become your joy . . . for all eternity.

God's goal is not to make you happy. It is to make you his.
Max Lucado

God's Gift of Family

You must choose for yourselves today whom
you will serve. . . . As for me and
my family, we will serve the Lord.

JOSHUA 24:15 NCV

Your family should be your biggest supporters and provide a safe place for you to come home to, but sometimes these close relationships are full of discord and grief. But if you're fortunate enough to have a loving and healthy family, hold tightly, even through frustration.

No family is perfect, including yours. But despite the inevitable challenges and hurt feelings of family life, your clan is God's gift to you. That little band of men, women, kids, and babies is a priceless treasure on temporary loan from the heavenly Father. Give thanks today for the gift of family. Enjoy the comfort of each other's presence. And determine that you and your family will serve the Lord.

*A man travels the world over in search
of what he needs, and returns home to find it.*

George Moore

A Bright Tomorrow

"I know what I am planning for you," says the
Lord. "I have good plans for you, not plans to hurt
you. I will give you hope and a good future."

JEREMIAH 29:11 NCV

God has wonderful plans for your bright future, even if you don't know what they are.

Still, the way you think about your future will play an important role in how your future unfolds. The phenomenon is called the "self-fulfilling prophecy"—what you predict will happen leads you to act in a certain way that causes that thing to happen.

Today, as you look to the future and make choices about how to live in the present, remember that God has an amazing plan for your bright tomorrow. Act—and believe—accordingly. And don't forget the sunglasses.

The future is as bright as the promises of God.
Adoniram Judson

Genuine Gratitude

I will give thanks to the Lord with all my heart; I will
tell of all Your wonders. I will be glad and exult in You;
I will sing praise to Your name, O Most High.

PSALM 9:1–2 NASB

We honor God, in part, by the genuine gratitude we feel
in our hearts for the blessings He has bestowed upon
us. Yet even the most saintly among us experiences periods of
apathy, times when we are not fully aware of or fully grateful
for the blessings and opportunities God has entrusted to our
care. Why? Because we're imperfect human beings who are in-
capable of perfect gratitude.

Even on life's darker days, we must make the effort to
cleanse our hearts of negative emotions and fill them, instead,
with praise, with love, with hope, and with thanksgiving.
When we do, we'll find an unexpected but undeniable comfort.
We may not have perfect gratitude, but we can know and express genuine gratitude.

*Contentment comes when we develop an attitude of
gratitude for the important things we do have in our
lives that we tend to take for granted if we have our
eyes staring longingly at our neighbor's stuff.*

Dave Ramsey

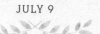

Patience and More Patience

> God blesses the people who patiently endure testing.
> Afterward they will receive the crown of life that
> God has promised to those who love Him.
>
> JAMES 1:12 NLT

Family life demands patience . . . and lots of it! We live in imperfect homes inhabited by imperfect people. Thank goodness family life doesn't have to be perfect to be wonderful!

Sometimes we inherit troubles from other folks (some of whom live under our roofs, and some who don't). On other occasions, we create trouble for ourselves. In either case, what's required is patience.

So here's a reminder: the next time you find your patience tested to the limit by the limitations of others, remember that nobody who inhabits your world is perfect (including you). And remember that the less you manage to focus on people's imperfections, the better for them and for you.

Patience achieves more than our force.
Edmund Burke

Love and Forgiveness

*When you are praying, first forgive anyone you
are holding a grudge against, so that your Father
in heaven will forgive your sins, too.*

MARK 11:25 NLT

Love and forgiveness are interconnected—when we have a relationship with God, one flows out of the other. Granting forgiveness when others hurt us is difficult, but not impossible.

God is willing to help you forgive others, but He also expects you to do some of the work. And make no mistake: forgiveness is work. It's not easy letting go of hurts or wrongs against us. God knows. He knows because He has suffered the wrongs and hurts we've inflicted on His heart. But we who know the comfort of His forgiveness should also be willing to share with others His gift of a love that forgives.

Forgiveness is the key to action and freedom.
Hannah Arendt

A Helping Hand

The greatest among you will be your servant.
For whoever exalts himself will be humbled, and
whoever humbles himself will be exalted.

MATTHEW 23:11–12 NIV

Jesus taught His followers about generosity. He taught that the most esteemed men and women should not be the self-congratulatory leaders of society, but rather the humblest of servants. If you were being graded on generosity, how would you score? Would you earn As in philanthropy and humility? If your grades could stand a little improvement, this is the perfect day to begin.

Today you may feel the urge to hoard your blessings. Don't do it. Instead, give generously to your neighbors, and do so without fanfare. Find a need and fill it . . . humbly. Lend a helping hand or share a word of kindness. Vow to do whatever it takes to improve your little corner of the world.

The world says that the more you take, the more you have.
Christ says, the more you give, the more you are.
Frederick Buechner

Growing Up Day by Day

The Message bears fruit and gets larger and stronger, just as it
has in you. From the very first day you heard and recognized
the truth of what God is doing, you've been hungry for more.

COLOSSIANS 1:6 MSG

Life is a grand and glorious classroom; school is always in session; and the rest is up to us. Every day provides opportunities to learn, to grow, and to share our wisdom with the world.

Sometimes God sends lessons disguised as problems. Sometimes He wraps His messages inside pain or loss or struggle or exhaustion. But no matter our circumstances, the Father never stops teaching. And if we're wise, we never stop looking for His lessons.

When it comes to your faith, God doesn't intend for you to stand still. He wants you to keep learning and growing every day of your life. No matter how "grown up" you may be, you still have growing to do. And the more you grow, the more beautiful you become, inside and out.

*Kindness in this world will do much to help others, not only
to come into the light, but also to grow in grace day by day.*
Fanny Crosby

The Art of Cooperation

Work at getting along with each other and with God.
Otherwise you'll never get so much as a glimpse of God.

HEBREWS 12:14 MSG

Have you learned the subtle art of cooperation? If so, you have learned the wisdom of give-and-take, not the foolishness of me-first. Cooperation is the art of compromising on many little things while keeping your eye on one big thing: your family.

But here's a word of warning: if you're like most folks, you're probably a little bit headstrong: you probably want most things done the way *you* want to do them. But, if you are observant, you will notice that people who always insist upon "my way or the highway" usually end up with "the highway."

A better strategy for all concerned (including you) is to abandon the search for "my way" and search instead for "our way." The happiest communities are those in which everybody learns how to give and take . . . with the emphasis on give.

Alone we can do so little; together we can do so much.
Helen Keller

Carried in His Hand

*I will be your God throughout your lifetime—until
your hair is white with age. I made you, and I will
care for you. I will carry you along and save you.*

ISAIAH 46:4 NLT

God has promised to lift you up and guide your steps if you'll follow Him. God has promised that when you entrust your life to Him completely, He will give you the strength to meet any challenge, the courage to face any trial, and the wisdom to live in His righteousness.

God's hand uplifts those who turn their hearts and prayers to Him. Will you count yourself among that number? Will you accept God's comfort and wear God's armor against the temptations and distractions of our troubled world? If you do, you can live courageously and optimistically, knowing that you are carried by the comforting, loving, unfailing hand of God.

*The God who spoke still speaks. He comes into our world.
He comes into your world. He comes to do what you can't.*

Max Lucado

Caring for Your Family

Each one of us needs to look after the good of the
people around us, asking ourselves, "How can I help?"

ROMANS 15:2 MSG

At times, family life can be challenging—and demanding.
Sometimes we wish we could withdraw from our responsibilities. But God has blessed us with families and He gives us
the opportunity to care for them.

As you think about your family today, ask yourself this
question: "How can I help?" Consider who in your clan—
including both your immediate and extended families—needs
a kind word, a heartfelt hug, a phone call, a letter, or even an
encouraging e-mail. Once you've decided who needs your
help, take action today to show care for that loved one.

No family is perfect, but your clan is God's gift to you.
They're a gift to be treasured. Today, give thanks for the many
ways you enjoy the care and comfort of a family . . . and then
offer that gift of care and comfort to them.

*The miraculous thing about being a family is that in the last
analysis, we are each dependent of one another and God,
woven together by mercy given and mercy received.*
Barbara Johnson

The Rewards of Courage

*Don't be afraid, because I am your God. I will
make you strong and will help you; I will support
you with my right hand that saves you.*

ISAIAH 41:10 NCV

Eleanor Roosevelt, niece of President Theodore Roosevelt and wife of President Franklin D. Roosevelt, accomplished much as America's longest-tenured First Lady. This remarkable woman offered first-class advice when she said, "You gain strength, courage, and confidence every time you look fear in the face."

If you're looking for a way to get more out of your life, consider any irrational fears that may be holding you back. Face up to your fear of failure (we all experience it) and refuse to back down in the face of adversity. And, most important, entrust your way to the God who has promised to strengthen and help you. When you do these things, you'll see that courage is its own reward . . . but not its only reward.

Nothing in life is to be feared. It is only to be understood.
Marie Curie

A Time to Grieve, a Time to Heal

They cried out to the Lord in their trouble, and
He saved them out of their distresses.

PSALM 107:13 NKJV

The book of Ecclesiastes reminds us that there is a time for everything—a time for grief and a time for healing (3:3–4). Even if you're currently gripped by an overwhelming sense of disappointment or loss, rest assured that better days are ahead. The Bible tells us that if we cry out to God, He will help and save us.

Is your relationship with the Creator such that you call out to Him when you're grieving? If not, are you willing to establish a personal, intimate relationship with Him? Are you willing to trust Him and depend on Him? If so, you'll come to know the indescribable comfort that grief, however devastating, is temporary, but that God's love is forever.

God stands ready to offer His healing hand. He's waiting for you to reach out to Him. So why not take His hand today?

In the soul-searching of our lives, we are to stay quiet so we
can hear Him say all that He wants to say to us in our hearts.
Charles Swindoll

Who Should You Trust?

*The one who understands a matter finds success, and
the one who trusts in the Lord will be happy.*

Proverbs 16:20 HCSB

Here's another question for you: where will you place your trust today? Will you trust in the ways of the world, or will you trust in the Word and the will of your Creator—who wants you to do great things for his kingdom.

Trusting God means trusting Him in every aspect of your life. You must trust Him with your relationships. You must trust Him with your finances. You must follow His commandments and pray for His guidance. Then you can wait patiently for God's revelations and for His blessings.

When you trust your heavenly Father, you can rest assured: in His own fashion and in His own time, God will bless you in ways you never could have imagined.

*God delights to meet the faith of one who looks up
to Him and says, "Lord, You know that I cannot
do this—but I believe that You can!"*

Amy Carmichael

A Day to Rejoice

Rejoice in the Lord, you righteous ones;
praise from the upright is beautiful.

PSALM 33:1 HCSB

This day is a blessed gift from God, and we have countless reasons to rejoice in it. Yet on some days, when the demands of life threaten to overwhelm us, we don't feel much like rejoicing. Instead of celebrating God's glorious creation, we may find ourselves wallowing in frustration and worried by uncertainties.

The familiar words of Psalm 118:24 remind us: "This is the day the Lord has made; let us rejoice and be glad in it" (NIV). Whatever this day holds for you, begin it and end it with God as your partner. Throughout the day, give thanks to the One who created you and saved you. God's love for you is infinite. What better reason to rejoice?

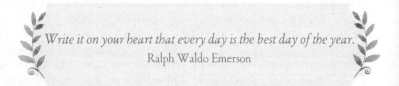

Write it on your heart that every day is the best day of the year.
Ralph Waldo Emerson

Good Work

There is nothing better for people than to be
happy in their work. That is why we are here!

ECCLESIASTES 3:22 NLT

S he acted in B movies and was cast in an old-time radio
program, but she was certainly no major star. But all that
changed when Lucille Ball, accompanied by her bandleader
husband Desi Arnaz, ventured into the then unproven medium
of television. When their show captured the hearts of fans everywhere, Lucy became an icon.

Fans the world over still enjoy reruns of *I Love Lucy*. The
show is fun to watch because it was fun to make. Lucy recalled,
"We had more fun on the set than we ever had at any party
after the show."

Doing good work can and should be a pleasure. So today,
imitate America's favorite redhead by weaving a little merri-
ment into your tasks. When you do good work and have fun
doing it, your star is sure to shine.

*To love what you do and feel that it matters—
how could anything be more fun?*
Katharine Graham

Waiting Quietly for God

I wait for the Lord; I wait, and put my hope in His word.

PSALM 130:5 HCSB

The Bible instructs us to wait quietly for the Lord, but as busy folks with too many obligations and too few hours in which to fulfill them, we find that waiting quietly for God can be difficult indeed. We know what we want and when we want it—sooner rather than later. But God operates according to His own perfect timetable. If we're wise, we will trust His plans—even when they differ from our own.

We would do well to be patient in all things. We must be patient with our families, our friends, and our associates. But we must also be patient with our Creator as He works out His plan for our lives. And that's as it should be. After all, think of how patient God has been with us.

The key to everything is patience.
You get the chicken by hatching the egg, not by smashing it.
Arnold Glasgow

Contentment That Lasts

Serving God does make us very rich, if we are satisfied
with what we have. We brought nothing into the
world, so we can take nothing out. But, if we have
food and clothes, we will be satisfied with that.

1 TIMOTHY 6:6–8 NCV

The preoccupation with happiness and contentment is ubiquitous in our world. But true contentment is a spiritual gift from God to those who trust in Him and follow His path.

Would you like to be a more contented person? Would you like to experience the kind of comfort and joy that money can never buy? Then don't depend on the world to make you happy, and don't expect material possessions to bring you real contentment. Contentment that lasts begins with God, so turn your thoughts and prayers to Him. You'll find you can be more than satisfied with that.

*The heart is rich when it is content, and it is always
content when its desires are set upon God.*
Saint Miguel of Ecuador

Do Something

Observe people who are good at their work—skilled
workers are always in demand and admired.

PROVERBS 22:29 MSG

Walter Cronkite quit school after his junior year at the University of Texas and began a series of newspaper reporting jobs. Thus began one of the most memorable journalistic careers in modern history. Cronkite was a war correspondent during World War II, and in time he became a fixture in American homes as the news anchor at CBS. A 1973 opinion poll even voted him the most trusted man in America.

Cronkite once observed, "I never had the ambition to be something. I had the ambition to do something." If you want to be someone special, don't aspire to public acclaim; aspire to excellence. Then, like Walter Cronkite, you'll discover that your audience is more likely to notice your work when you let that work speak for itself.

Excellence is not an act but a habit. The things you
do the most are the things you will do best.
Marva Collins

Comforting Friends

As iron sharpens iron, so a friend sharpens a friend.
PROVERBS 27:17 NLT

Where can we turn for comfort? Loyal friends have much to offer us—encouragement, faith, fellowship, fun, and understanding, for starters. Throughout the Bible, God reminds us to love one another, to care for one another, and to treat one another as we wish to be treated. When we live by God's Golden Rule, we help build His kingdom here on earth.

Today, resolve to be a trustworthy, encouraging, and loyal friend—and treasure the people in your life who are loyal friends to you. Friendship is a glorious gift, provided and blessed by God. Give thanks for that gift and nurture it.

Friendship plays an important role in God's plan for His world and for your life. He blesses you through your friends and if you let Him; He'll use you to bless your friends as well.

Christ . . . can truly say to every group of Christian friends, "Ye have not chosen one another but I have chosen you for one another."
C. S. Lewis

A Clear Conscience

*Let us come near to God with a sincere heart and a sure faith,
because we have been made free from a guilty conscience,
and our bodies have been washed with pure water.*

Hebrews 10:22 NCV

Few things in life provide more comfort than a clear conscience. In fact, a clear conscience is one of the undeniable blessings we receive whenever we allow God to guide our path through the trials and temptations of everyday life.

Have you formed the habit of listening carefully to that still, small voice of God's Spirit? That little voice has much to teach us about the decisions we make and the way we choose to live.

Today, as you make the myriad decisions about what you do and say, let the Spirit's voice be your guide. When you do, you'll enjoy the refreshing feeling of having a clear conscience before God.

*To go against one's conscience is neither safe
nor right. Here I stand; I cannot do otherwise.*
Martin Luther

Your Mission

*Be strong and courageous, and do the work. Do not be afraid
or discouraged, for the Lord God, my God, is with you.*

1 CHRONICLES 28:20 NIV

F red Rogers was an ordained minister who wrote more than
two hundred songs, but he will forever be remembered as
the beloved friend and mentor to millions of children—the
soft-spoken television icon who created *Mister Rogers' Neighborhood.*

Rogers observed, "Each of us has only one life on this
earth, and we should use it."

Fred Rogers followed his own advice, and so should you.
God created you for a purpose, and He'll do His part to help
you find and fulfill it. In turn, He asks you to make your life a
mission, not an intermission. So get busy. You have important
work to do in your neighborhood.

*Whatever purpose motivates your life,
it must be something big enough and grand enough
to make the investment worthwhile.*
Warren Wiersbe

Enthusiastic Discipleship

*Do your work with enthusiasm. Work as if you were serving
the Lord, not as if you were serving only men and women.*

EPHESIANS 6:7 NCV

With whom will you choose to walk today? Will you walk
with shortsighted people who honor the ways of the
world, or will you walk with the Son of God? Jesus wants to
walk with you. Will you choose to walk with Him today, and
every day of your life?

Jesus has called on people of every generation to follow in
His footsteps. And He promised that when we do, our burdens
will be light (Matthew 11:28–30).

Jesus doesn't want you to be a run-of-the-mill, follow-
the-crowd kind of person. He wants you to be a "new creation"
through Him. And that's the best thing you could want for
yourself. Today, undertake each task enthusiastically, remembering that you do it not just for others but for God. Then
you'll know the joy of discipleship.

*Being a disciple involves becoming
a learner, a student of the Master.*
Charles Stanley

Heeding God's Call

You did not choose me, but I chose you and appointed
you to go and bear fruit—fruit that will last.

JOHN 15:16 NIV

God is calling you to follow a specific path that He has cho-sen for your life. And it is vitally important that you heed that call. Otherwise, your talents may not reach their full po-tential, and precious opportunities may be lost forever.

Have you already heard God's call? Are you pursuing it with vigor? If so, you're both blessed and wise. But if you have not yet discovered what God intends for you to do with your life, keep searching and praying. And in the meantime, con-tinue to love others and share God's message.

Remember that God has important work for you to do—work designed specifically for you. He has placed you in a partic-ular location, amid selected people, with unique opportunities to serve. And He will give you all the tools you need to succeed. So listen for His voice, watch for His leading, and step out in faith to heed His call.

*The place where God calls you to is the place where your
deep gladness and the world's deep hunger meet.*
Frederick Buechner

To God Be the Glory

God is against the proud, but he gives grace to the humble.

1 PETER 5:5 NCV

Would you like to enjoy a more peaceful, grace-filled life? Then spend more time meditating on God's greatness than on your own. Contemplate your blessings and be sure to give credit where credit is due—to your Creator.

Dietrich Bonhoeffer said, "It is very easy to overestimate the importance of our own achievements in comparison with what we owe others." We are imperfect human beings who sometimes like to inflate our accomplishments.

But reality breeds humility. When we see ourselves in light of God's glory, we realize that He alone is worthy of praise. Instead of puffing out our chests and saying "Look at us!" we should give glory to God. When we do, we'll know the incomparable comfort of His grace poured out on our hearts and lives.

What makes humility so desirable is the marvelous thing it does to us; it creates in us a capacity for the closest possible intimacy with God.

Monica Baldwin

A Dose of Laughter

A happy heart is like good medicine.

PROVERBS 17:22 NCV

Laughter is medicine for the soul, but sometimes, amid the stresses of the day, we forget to take it. Instead of viewing our world with a mixture of optimism and humor, we allow worries and distractions to rob us of the joy God intends for our lives.

So the next time you find yourself dwelling on the negatives of life, refocus your attention to things positive. The next time you fall prey to the blight of pessimism, turn your mind to happier thoughts.

With God, your glass is never half empty. With God as your companion and eternal hope, your glass is really full and overflowing. With Him, you can have a happy heart. So today, seek out things that tickle your funny bone—and laugh.

Mirth is God's medicine. Everybody ought to bathe in it.
Henry Ward Beecher

Happy Day

How happy is everyone who fears the
Lord, who walks in His ways!

PSALM 128:1 HCSB

All too often, people think of happiness as an emotion they felt in the past or something they may experience someday in the distant future—but they're mistaken. Happiness lives in the present tense; happiness can be found in each precious moment.

Are you willing to celebrate your life today? After all, this day—and each moment in it—is a blessed gift from God. When you stop to think about it, you probably have many reasons to rejoice.

So whatever this day holds for you, know that it can be a happy day when you trust God and follow Him. Throughout this day, give thanks to the One Who created you. God's love for you is infinite. Accept it joyfully . . . and be happy.

*Men spend their lives in anticipation, in determining
to be vastly happy at some period or other,
when they have time. The present time has one
advantage over every other: it is our own.*
Charles Caleb Colton

AUGUST

Discovering Wholeness

If your sinful nature controls your mind, there is death. But if the Holy Spirit controls your mind, there is life and peace.

ROMANS 8:6 NLT

Until we open our hearts to God, we are never completely whole. Until we have placed our hearts and our lives firmly in the hands of our loving heavenly Father, we are incomplete. Until we discover the peace that passes all understanding—the peace that God promises can and should be ours—we long for a sense of wholeness that continues to elude us no matter how diligently we search.

It is only through God that we discover lasting peace. We may search far and wide for worldly substitutes, but when we seek peace apart from God, we will find neither peace nor God.

Today, lay claim to the peace that really matters: Your Creator's. And then share it—today, tomorrow, and every day that you live.

Jesus knows one of the greatest barriers to our faith is often our unwillingness to be made whole—our unwillingness to accept responsibility—our unwillingness to live without excuse for our spiritual smallness and immaturity.

Anne Graham Lotz

Don't Expect Them to Be Perfect

Those who show mercy to others are happy,
because God will show mercy to them.
MATTHEW 5:7 NCV

No one is perfect—not you, and not the people that you care about the most. But despite their imperfections, every single member of your family (and those you consider family) is a unique gift from the Creator. And you should treat His gifts with the care and respect they deserve. So refrain from the temptation to lecture or scold. Be slow to anger and quick to forgive. Put an end to negativity; focus, to the best of your abilities, on the positive, and know what to overlook.

The next time a member of your clan makes a mistake, don't criticize or complain. Instead, make it a point to forgive and forget as quickly as possible. Until the day that you become perfect, don't expect others to be.

Do not think of the faults of others
but of what is good in them and faulty in yourself.
Saint Teresa of Àvila

Getting Excited About Today

This is the day which the Lord has made;
let us rejoice and be glad in it.

PSALM 118:24 NASB

Are you looking forward to the coming day with a mixture of anticipation and excitement? Or are you a little less enthused than that?

We all know that some days are filled with sweetness and light, while other days aren't. But even on the darker days of life, you have much to celebrate—including, but not limited to, your life and your loved ones.

As a citizen of the world, you have incredibly important work to do. And you have a vitally important message to share with your family. Share that message with gusto. Your family needs your enthusiasm, and you deserve the rewards that will be yours when you share your wisdom enthusiastically and often.

*Man's mind is not a container to be filled
but rather a fire to be kindled.*
Dorothea Brande

The Power of Kindness

God has chosen you and made you his holy people.
He loves you. So always do these things: Show mercy
to others, be kind, humble, gentle, and patient.

COLOSSIANS 3:12 NCV

Never underestimate the power of kindness. You never know what small word or gesture will significantly change someone's day or week or life.

Is your home a place "where never is heard a discouraging word and the skies are not cloudy all day" . . . or is the forecast slightly cloudier than that? If your corner of the world is a place where the rule of the day is the Golden Rule, don't change a thing. Kindness starts at home, but it should never end there.

So today, slow down and be alert for those who need your smile, your kind words, or your helping hand. Make kindness the centerpiece of your dealings with others. They will be blessed, and so will you.

Sometimes one little spark of kindness is all it takes to reignite the light of hope in a heart that's blinded by pain.
Barbara Johnson

Watch the Ants

Go watch the ants, you lazy person. Watch what they do and be wise. Ants have no commander, no leader or ruler, but they store up food in the summer and gather their supplies at harvest. How long will you lie there, you lazy person? When will you get up from sleeping?

PROVERBS 6:6–9 NCV

The Bible instructs us that we can learn an important lesson from a surprising source: ants. Ants are among nature's most industrious creatures. They do their work without supervision and without hesitation.

God's Word is clear: We are instructed to work diligently and faithfully. We are told that the fields are ripe for the harvest, that the workers are few, and that the importance of our work is profound. Let us labor, then, without hesitation and without complaint. Nighttime is coming. Until it does, let us honor our heavenly Father with grateful hearts and willing hands.

It is our best work that God wants, not the dregs of our exhaustion. I think he must prefer quality to quantity.
George MacDonald

Strength for the Struggle

O Lord, you are my lamp. The Lord lights up my darkness.

2 SAMUEL 22:29 NLT

Life is a tapestry of good days and bad days. When the good days predominate, it's easy to take our blessings for granted (a temptation we must resist with all our might). But during life's difficult days, we discover precisely what we're made of. And, more importantly, we discover what our faith is made of.

Has your faith been put to the test? With God's help, you can endure life's darker days. Remembering that is important, because when your faith is again put to the test—as it likely will be—you can rest assured that God is perfectly willing, and always ready, to give you strength for the struggle.

The ultimate measure of a man is not where he stands in moments of comfort and convenience, but where he stands at times of challenge and controversy.

Martin Luther King Jr.

Living in Our Material World

Let us lay aside every weight and the sin that so easily ensnares us, and run with endurance the race that lies before us, keeping our eyes on Jesus, the source and perfecter of our faith.

HEBREWS 12:1–2 HCSB

On the grand stage of a well-lived life, material possessions should play a rather small role. Of course, we all need the basic necessities of life. But once we meet those needs for ourselves and for our families, the piling up of possessions creates more problems than it solves. Our real riches, of course, are not of this world. We are never really rich until we are rich in spirit.

Do you sometimes find yourself wrapped up in the concerns of the material world? You're not the only person in your neighborhood to do so. Thankfully, the trap of materialism is a trap you can escape by turning your thoughts and your prayers to more important matters. When you do, you'll begin storing spiritual riches that will endure throughout eternity.

Since my money is God's money, every spending decision I make is a spiritual decision.
John Hagee

Seeking His Wisdom

Does not wisdom call out? Does not understanding
raise her voice? On the heights along the way,
where the paths meet, she takes her stand.

PROVERBS 8:1–2 NIV

D o you seek wisdom for yourself and for your family? As
a thoughtful person living in a society that is filled with
temptations and distractions, you know that it's all too easy
to stray far from the source of ultimate wisdom: God's Holy
Word.

When you commit yourself to daily study of God's
Word—and when you live according to His commandments—
you will become wise . . . in time. But don't expect to open your
Bible today and be wise tomorrow. Acquiring wisdom takes
patience.

Today and every day, as a way of understanding God's
plan for your life, study His Word and live by it. When you do,
you will accumulate a storehouse of wisdom that will enrich
your own life and the lives of your family members, your
friends, and the world.

*Knowledge can be learned, but wisdom must be
earned. Wisdom is knowledge . . . lived.*
Sheila Walsh

Caring for the Downtrodden

*Whatever you did for one of the least of these
brothers of mine, you did for me.*

MATTHEW 25:40 NIV

How fortunate we are to live in a land of opportunities and possibilities. But for many people around the world—and even in our own backyard—the kind of opportunities we enjoy are scarce. In too many parts of the globe, hardworking men and women struggle merely to provide food and shelter for their families.

Because much has been given to us, much is expected. Because so many material blessings have been entrusted to our care, we should be quick to share our possessions with others, wherever they are.

When we care for the downtrodden, and when we show compassion for those who suffer, we follow the instructions of the One Who created us. What sweet comfort and joy to know that what we do for others, we do for God.

*How wonderful it is that nobody need wait a single
moment before starting to improve the world.*
Anne Frank

Celebrating Others

*Let us think about each other and help each
other to show love and do good deeds.*

HEBREWS 10:24 NCV

Each day provides countless opportunities to encourage others and to praise their good works. When we do that, we not only spread seeds of joy and happiness, we also follow the commandments of God's Holy Word.

It takes little effort to share a kind word or a compliment with the people in your life. A small phrase from you could turn a whole day around.

Today, look for the good in others—starting with your family members. And then celebrate the good that you find. When you do, you'll be a powerful force of encouragement in your corner of the world . . . and an enduring blessing to others.

*The greatest good you can do for another is not just to
share your riches, but to reveal to him his own.*
Benjamin Disraeli

God's Surprising Plans for You

*I will guide you along the best pathway for your
life. I will advise you and watch over you.*

PSALM 32:8 NLT

God's Word indicates that when we do our duties in small matters, He will give us additional responsibilities (Matthew 25:14–21). Sometimes these responsibilities come when God changes the course of our lives so that we may better serve Him. Sometimes our rewards come in the form of temporary setbacks that lead, in turn, to greater victories. Sometimes God rewards us by saying no to our requests so that He can say yes to a far grander gift that we, in our limited understanding, would never have thought to ask for.

If you seek to be God's servant in great matters, be faithful, be patient, and be dutiful in smaller matters. Then step back and watch as God surprises you with the spectacular creativity of His infinite wisdom and His perfect plan.

Every man's life is a plan of God.
Horace Bushnell

Strength for the Day

The Lord is a refuge for His people and a stronghold.

JOEL 3:16 NASB

Have you made God the cornerstone of your life, or is He relegated to a few hours on Sunday morning? Have you genuinely allowed God to reign over every corner of your heart, or have you attempted to place Him in a limited "spiritual compartment?"

When you trust God with your life, you'll find that He's a refuge and a source of strength you can turn to throughout your day and throughout your life.

God loves you. In times of trouble, He will comfort you; in times of sorrow, He will dry your tears. When you are weak or sorrowful, remember that God is as near as your next breath. He stands at the door of your heart, waiting and longing for your invitation. Welcome Him in and trust Him to guide you. Today, accept the peace, the strength, and the comfort that only God can give.

*In my weakness, I have learned, like Moses,
to lean hard on God. The weaker I am, the harder I
lean on Him. The harder I lean, the stronger I discover
Him to be. The stronger I discover God to be, the more
resolute I am in this job He's given me to do.*
Joni Eareckson Tada

Simple Wisdom

*Don't abandon wisdom, and she will watch over
you; love her, and she will guard you.*

<small>PROVERBS 4:6 HCSB</small>

Robert Fulghum's most popular book was titled *All I Really Need to Know I Learned in Kindergarten*. As the title makes clear, Fulghum's philosophy isn't comprised of complex philosophies or obtuse truisms. He observed, "What's necessary to live a meaningful life—that isn't all that complicated. . . . Wisdom was not at the top of the graduate-school mountain, but there in the sandpile at Sunday School."

If you're looking for a surefire way to improve your life, try the advice Fulghum offers in his book. Follow the rules you learned as a kid: be polite, tell the truth, clean up your messes, play fair, and do the right thing. You'll discover that being a responsible grown-up is not as complicated as it seems. In fact, sometimes it's as simple as child's play.

Everything should be made as simple as possible.
Albert Einstein

When Mistakes Become Lessons

The one who conceals his sins will not prosper, but
whoever confesses and renounces them will find mercy.

PROVERBS 28:13 HCSB

We are imperfect people living in an imperfect world; mistakes are simply part of the price we pay for being here. But even though mistakes are an inevitable part of life's journey, repeated mistakes should not be. When we commit the inevitable blunders of life, we must correct them, learn from them, and pray to God for the wisdom not to repeat them. And then, if we are successful, our mistakes become lessons, and our lives become adventures in growth, not stagnation.

So the next time you experience one of life's inevitable setbacks, it's time to start looking for the lesson that God is trying to teach you. It's time to learn what needs to be learned, change what needs to be changed, and move on.

*We ought not to look back unless it is to derive
useful lessons from past errors and for the purpose
of profiting by dearly bought experience.*
George Washington

The Importance of Words

*From a wise mind comes wise speech; the
words of the wise are persuasive.*

PROVERBS 16:23 NLT

The words we speak are more important than we may realize. Our words have echoes that extend beyond place or time. If our words are encouraging, we can lift others up; if our words are hurtful, we can hold others back.

So here's a pair of questions for you to consider: Are you a source of encouragement to the people you encounter every day? And are you careful to speak words that lift those people up? If so, you will avoid angry outbursts. You will refrain from impulsive outpourings. You will terminate tantrums. Instead, you will speak words of encouragement and hope to friends, to family members, to coworkers, and even to strangers. They, like just about everybody else in the world, need all the hope and encouragement they can get.

*Attitude and the spirit in which we communicate
are as important as the words we say.*
Charles Stanley

Showing God's Love

Beloved, if God so loved us, we also ought to love one another.

1 JOHN 4:11 NASB

Love begins and ends with God, but the middle part belongs to us. During the brief time that we have here on earth, God has given each of us the opportunity to become a loving person, to be kind, to be courteous, to be cooperative, and to be forgiving—to obey the Golden Rule. Unfortunately, sometimes we try to make up our own rules as we go.

If we choose to reject the many opportunities God has given us to show love to others, we cheat ourselves out of His incomparable rewards.

The decisions we make, and the results of those decisions, affect the quality of our relationships. God has taken the first step: He loved us even before we loved Him. Today, choose to show love not only to your heavenly Father, but also to those He has placed in your path.

When you reach the point where the happiness, security, and development of another person is as much of a driving force to you as your own happiness, security, and development, then you have a mature love. True love is spelled G-I-V-E.
Josh McDowell

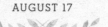

Beyond Materialism

What will it profit a man if he gains the whole world, and loses his own soul? Or what will a man give in exchange for his soul?
MARK 8:36–37 NKJV

In modern society, we need money to live. But if we're wise, we'll never make the acquisition of money the central focus of our lives. Money is a tool, but it should never overwhelm our sensibilities. Our focus should be on things spiritual, not things material. Yet the world encourages us to do the opposite.

The world glorifies material possessions, but God values our souls. Whenever we place our love for material possessions above our love for God, we make ourselves less comfortable, less contented, less satisfied with life. We do harm to our souls.

So today, free yourself from the chains of materialism. Nourish your soul by moving beyond the material to the spiritual. Peace and comfort are waiting for you there.

Keeping up with the Joneses is like keeping up with a scared jackrabbit—only harder.
Marie T. Freeman

He Reigns

In all your ways acknowledge Him, and
He shall direct your paths.

PROVERBS 3:6 NKJV

God is sovereign. He reigns over the entire universe, and He's directing your little corner of the world, too. Your challenge is to recognize God's sovereignty and live in accordance with His directions. Of course, sometimes this is easier said than done.

Your heavenly Father may not always reveal His will as quickly (or as clearly) as you'd like. But rest assured: God is in control. He is right here with you and He wants to use you in wonderful, exciting ways.

Today, as you fulfill the responsibilities of everyday life, keep God in first place. When you do, He'll lead you along a path of His choosing. You need only watch, listen, learn . . . and follow.

*Sovereignty means that ultimately God alone has
the right to declare what creation should be.*
Stanley Grenz

Seeking God's Will

Teach me to do Your will, for You are my God; Your Spirit is good. Lead me in the land of uprightness.

God has a plan for our world and for our lives. The Creator does nothing by accident; He is willful and intentional. Unfortunately for us, we cannot always understand the will of the Father. Why? Because we are mortal beings with limited understanding. Although we cannot fully comprehend the will of God, we should always trust it.

As this day unfolds, seek to know God's will and to obey His instructions. When you entrust your life to Him without reservation, He will give you wisdom, courage, and comfort. So don't wait another day—seek God's will today. Follow His lead. Trust His guidance, and accept His love. His Spirit is good, and His will is to lead you to a land of uprightness . . . and eternal blessing.

"If the Lord will" is not just a statement on a believer's lips; it is the constant attitude of his heart.
Warren Wiersbe

A Helping Hand

The Samaritan . . . put the hurt man on his own donkey
and took him to an inn where he cared for him.

LUKE 10:33–34 NCV

Sometimes we'd like to help make the world a better place,
but we're not sure how to do it. Jesus told the story of the
good Samaritan, a man who cared for a fellow traveler when no
one else would. He told this story to show that we, too, should
lend a hand when we encounter people who need our help.

When bad things happen in our world, there's always
something we can do. What can you do today to make God's
world a better place? You can start by making your own corner
of the world a little happier by sharing kind words and good
deeds. And when you become aware of people's needs—and
you've done what you can to meet those needs—take those
concerns to God in prayer. Whether you've offered a helping
hand or a heartfelt prayer, you've done more than you think.

*Make it a rule, and pray to God to help you to keep it,
never, if possible, to lie down at night without being able to
say: "I have made one human being at least a little wiser,
or a little happier, or at least a little better this day."*

Charles Kingsley

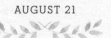

Look Before You Leap

*An impulsive vow is a trap; later you'll
wish you could get out of it.*

PROVERBS 20:25 MSG

Are you sometimes just a little too impulsive? Do you occasionally leap before you look? If so, you may find it helpful (and ultimately comforting) to take a careful look at what the Bible says about impulsiveness.

In Proverbs we are taught to be thoughtful, not reckless. Yet the world often tempts us to behave recklessly. Sometimes we're faced with powerful temptations to be impulsive, undisciplined. These are temptations we must resist.

When you make a habit of thinking first and acting second, you'll be comforted in the knowledge that you're incorporating God's wisdom into the fabric of your life. And you'll reap the rewards the Creator bestows on wise folks (like you) who take the time to look—and think—before they leap.

Delay is preferable to error.
Thomas Jefferson

Your Spiritual Health

I love you, O Lord, my strength.

PSALM 18:1 NIV

In order to become more spiritually healthy, we must—as C. S. Lewis noted in *The Four Loves*—refocus on the depth of our love for God, as well as his for us. We do that partly when we worship Him and obey Him.

When we worship God faithfully and obediently, we invite His love into our hearts. When we truly serve God, by allowing Him to rule over our days and our lives, we'll sense His presence and His love for us. That, in turn, leads us to grow to love God even more deeply.

Today, open your heart to the Father. When you do, your spiritual health will improve . . . and so will every other aspect of your life.

He who is filled with love is filled with God Himself.
Saint Augustine

Your Spiritual Journey

Leave inexperience behind, and you will live;
pursue the way of understanding.

PROVERBS 9:6 HCSB

Gaining spiritual maturity takes time. No one among us possesses the insight or the discipline to become instant saints. And that's perfectly okay with God. He understands that none of us is perfect and that we all have room for personal, emotional, and spiritual growth.

Life is a series of decisions. When we live according to the principles contained in God's Word, we embark on a journey toward spiritual maturity that results in life abundant and life eternal.

Are you feeling less than perfect today? If so, don't fret. You don't have to be perfect to follow God. And even though you'll never achieve complete spiritual maturity in this lifetime, you can still keep growing—today and every day. When you do, the results will be wonderful.

You've got to continue to grow, or you're just like
last night's corn bread—stale and dry.
Loretta Lynn

Don't Worry About Tomorrow

Seek first his kingdom and his righteousness, and all
these things will be given to you as well. Therefore do
not worry about tomorrow, for tomorrow will worry
about itself. Each day has enough trouble of its own.

MATTHEW 6:33–34 NIV

You may on occasion find yourself worrying about health,
finances, safety, relationships, family, and countless
other challenges of life, some great and some small. Take your
worries to God. And after you've talked to God, it also helps to
talk openly to the people who love you, the trusted friends and
family members who know you best. The more you talk and
the more you pray, the better you'll feel.

Once you've talked things over with friends, family,
and God, it's time to get busy fixing what's broken. So instead of worrying about tomorrow, do today's work and
leave the rest up to God. When you do, you'll discover that
if you do your part today, the future has a way of taking
care of itself.

*Remember always that there are two things which
are more utterly incompatible even than oil and
water, and these two are trust and worry.*
Hannah Whitall Smith

Pause for Praise

Praise the Lord. Give thanks to the Lord, for
He is good; His love endures forever.
PSALM 106:1 NIV

Sometimes, in our rush to get things done, we don't stop long enough to pause and thank our Creator for the countless blessings He has bestowed upon us. After all, we're busy people with many demands on our time; we have so much to do. But when we slow down long enough to express our gratitude to the One who made us, we enrich our own lives and the lives of those around us.

Thanksgiving should become a habit, a regular part of our daily routines. God has blessed us beyond measure and we owe Him everything, including our time and praise.

So today, pause and count your blessings. Then give thanks to the Giver of every good gift. God's love for you is never-ending; your praise for Him should be never-ending, too.

Be not afraid of saying too much in the praises
of God; all the danger is of saying too little.
Matthew Henry

Solving Problems

People who do what is right may have many
problems, but the Lord will solve them all.

PSALM 34:19 NCV

Life is an exercise in problem solving. The question is not whether or not we will encounter problems; the question is how we will choose to address them. When it comes to solving the problems of everyday living, we often know precisely what needs to be done, but we may be slow in doing it—especially if what needs to be done is difficult or uncomfortable for us. So we put off till tomorrow what should be done today.

The words of Psalm 34 remind us that the Lord solves problems for "people who do what is right." And usually, doing what's right means doing the uncomfortable work of confronting our problems sooner rather than later. What problems do you have today? Do what's right, and take them to the Lord. He'll help you solve them.

*If you simply let a problem wash around in your
mind, it will seem greater, and much more vague,
than it will appear on close examination.*
Dorothea Brande

Depending upon God

*It will come about that whoever calls on the
name of the Lord will be delivered.*

JOEL 2:32 NASB

God is a never-ending source of strength and courage if we call upon Him. When we are weary, He gives us strength. When we see no hope, God reminds us of His promises. When we grieve, God wipes away our tears.

Do you feel overwhelmed by the responsibilities of today? Are you mired in yesterday's regrets? Or do you feel pressured by the uncertainty of tomorrow? If so, then turn your concerns and your prayers over to God. He knows your needs, and He has promised to meet those needs. Whatever your circumstances, God will protect you and care for you . . . if you let Him. Invite Him into your heart and allow Him to renew your spirit. When you trust in Him, He will never fail you.

*A car is made to run on gasoline, and it would not
run properly on anything else. . . . God desgined
the human machine to run on Himself.*

C. S. Lewis

Under Control

People may make plans in their minds, but
the Lord decides what they will do.

PROVERBS 16:9 NCV

I f you're like most people, you like being in control. You want
things to happen according to your wishes and your timetable. But sometimes God has other plans—and, ultimately, He
will have the final word.

If you've encountered unfortunate circumstances that are
beyond your control, trust God, who *is* in control. When you
place your faith in Him, you can be comforted in the knowledge that He is both loving and wise, and that He understands
His plans perfectly, even when you do not.

*Acceptance is resting in God's goodness, believing
that He has all things under His control.*
Charles Swindoll

Learning to Live in the Future Tense

Wisdom is pleasing to you. If you find it,
you have hope for the future.

PROVERBS 24:14 NCV

C an you find the courage to accept the past by forgiving all those who have injured you (including yourself)? If you can, you can then look to the future with a sense of optimism and hope.

God has instructed you to place your hopes in Him, and He has promised that you will be His throughout eternity. Your task is to take God at His Word.

Of course, we all face occasional disappointments and failures while we are here on earth, but these are only temporary defeats. This world can be a place of trials and tribulations, but we are secure. God has promised us peace, joy, and eternal life. And God keeps His promises today, tomorrow, and forever.

For what has been, thanks! For what shall be, yes!
Dag Hammarskjöld

Pushing Past Procrastination

*If you make a promise to God, don't be slow to keep it.
God is not happy with fools, so give God what you promised.*

<small>ECCLESIASTES 5:4 NCV</small>

If you've acquired the habit of putting off until tomorrow what needs to be done today, you know how terrible procrastination can make you feel. So if you'd like to feel a little better about yourself, try this: make it a habit to do things in the order of their importance, not in the order of your preference. When you do, you'll discover how good it feels to finish the difficult work first, rather than putting it off until the last possible minute.

Once you acquire the habit of doing first things first, you'll dramatically reduce your stress. You'll be more productive. You'll even sleep better at night.

So learn to defeat procrastination by focusing on the big rewards you'll receive when you finish your work. It's the productive—and the peaceful—way to live.

*Don't duck the most difficult problems. That just ensures that
the hardest part will be left when you're most tired.
Get the big one done—it's all downhill from then on.*

Norman Vincent Peale

When the World Demands Perfection

*A devout life does bring wealth, but it's the rich
simplicity of being yourself before God.*

1 TIMOTHY 6:6 MSG

Face it: sometimes it can be tough to respect yourself, especially if you're feeling like a less-than-perfect citizen living in a world that seems to demand perfection. But before you plunge headlong into self-critical thoughts, consider this: God knows all your imperfections, all your faults, and all your shortcomings . . . and He loves you anyway. And because God loves you, you can—and should—feel good about the person you see when you look in the mirror.

God's love is bigger and more powerful than anyone (even you) can imagine, but it's no fairy tale; His love is real. So do yourself a favor today: accept God's love with open arms. Whenever you have a moment when you don't love yourself very much, stop and remember this: God does loves you . . . a lot. And God is always right.

When everything has to be right, something isn't.
Stanislaw Lec

SEPTEMBER

Feeling Good About Your Abilities

There are varieties of gifts, but the same Spirit. And there are varieties of ministries, and the same Lord.

1 CORINTHIANS 12:4–5 NASB

God has given each of us gifts. You have an array of talents, some of which you've refined, but some of them still need work. But nobody will force you to do the hard work of converting raw skill into prime-time talent. It's a job you must do for yourself. That may sound difficult, but the truth is, you'll feel better about yourself when you hone your abilities.

Today, make a promise to yourself and to your Creator that you will earnestly seek to discover and refine the talents He has given you. Ask Him to help you nourish those talents and make them grow. And then get down to the business of why you were blessed with such abilities to begin with; vow to share your gifts with the world for as long as God gives you the power to do so.

When I stand before God at the end of my life, I would hope that I would not have a single bit of talent left, and could say, "I used everything You gave me."
Erma Bombeck

Strength for Today

Those who hope in the Lord will renew their strength.
They will soar on wings like eagles; they will run and
not grow weary, they will walk and not be faint.

ISAIAH 40:31 NIV

Where do you go to find strength? The gym? The health food store? The espresso bar? The ice cream shop? These places are all fine, but there's a better source of strength—God. He will be a never-ending source of power and courage if you call upon Him.

Are you energized? Have you tapped in to God's strength? Have you turned your life and your heart over to Him, or are you still muddling along under your own power? The answer to these questions will determine the quality of your day and your life. So start tapping in—and remember that when it comes to strength, God is the Ultimate Source.

As we join together in prayer,
we draw on God's enabling might in a way
that multiplies our own efforts many times over.
Shirley Dobson

Rejoicing Hearts

Let the hearts of those who seek the Lord rejoice. Look to the Lord and his strength; seek his face always.

1 Chronicles 16:10–11 NIV

What is your attitude today? Are you fearful or worried? Are you more concerned about pleasing your friends than about pleasing your God? Are you bitter, confused, cynical, or pessimistic? If so, it's time to have a little chat with your Father in heaven.

God wants to fill your life with spiritual abundance and joy—but He won't force His joy upon you. You must claim it for yourself. So today, do yourself this favor: accept God's gifts with a smile on your face, a song on your lips, and joy in your heart.

Think optimistically about yourself and your future. And share this encouragement with others who may need comfort. Then together, your hearts can rejoice as you praise your Father in heaven and thank Him for His gifts. After all, He has already given you so much . . . and He wants to give you so much more.

There is not one blade of grass, there is no color in this world that is not intended to make us rejoice.

John Calvin

When Behavior Reflects Belief

Teach me, O Lord, the way of Your statutes, and I shall keep it to the end. Give me understanding, and I shall keep Your law; indeed, I shall observe it with my whole heart.

PSALM 119:33–34 NKJV

When we act in accordance with our beliefs—beliefs we've built on the foundation of God's Word—we inevitably feel more comfortable with our decisions. Why? Because we know intuitively, as well as from experience, that sound, biblically based convictions will not lead us astray.

When you listen carefully to the quiet voice of God deep within your heart, you will make good choices. So as you decide how to respond to the ups and downs of daily living, be sure to stop long enough (and early enough) to listen to God's whispered direction. Then put your faith in motion by making sure your words and your actions line up with the principles of your firm faith. You'll then have the comfort of knowing that with God as your Counselor, you can take the next step with confidence.

Conscience is God's lamp within the human breast.
Billy Graham

Rejoice!

Rejoice in the Lord always. Again I will say, rejoice!
PHILIPPIANS 4:4 NKJV

Have you made the choice to rejoice? Do you seek happiness, comfort, and contentment? The way to find all of those things is to rejoice—after all, your life is a gift from God, a blessing to be savored and celebrated. And the best day to begin that celebration is this one.

What does life have in store for you? A world full of possibilities (if you'll have faith enough to embrace them) and God's promise of peace and joy (if you'll trust Him enough to accept them). So as you embark upon the next phase of your journey, remember to celebrate the life God has given you. Your Creator has blessed you beyond measure. Honor Him with your prayers, your words, your deeds, and your joy.

The spiritual life is a life beyond moods. It is a life in which we choose joy and do not allow ourselves to become victims of passing feelings of happiness or depression.
Henri Nouwen

The Anchor

We have this [hope]—like a sure and firm anchor of the
soul—that enters the inner sanctuary behind the curtain.
HEBREWS 6:19 HCSB

D o you feel as though the ground is trembling beneath your
feet? Seek stability by standing on the firm foundation of
faith.

The same God Who created the universe will protect you
and be your sanctuary if you just ask Him to . . . so ask, and
then serve Him with willing hands and a trusting heart.

Today and every day, you can rest assured that although
the world may change moment by moment, God's love endures—unfathomable and unchanging—forever. Let God's
love be the anchor of your soul.

*When did God's love for you begin? When He began
to be God. When did He begin to be God? Never, for
He has always been without beginning and without
end, and so He has always loved you from eternity.*
Saint Francis of Sales

Knowing and Pleasing God

*Here's how we can be sure that we know God in
the right way: Keep his commandments.*

1 JOHN 2:2–3 MSG

In order to enjoy a deeper relationship with God, we must strive diligently to live in accordance with His commandments. But there's a problem—we live in a world that seeks to snare our attention and lead us away from the Creator.

Because we are imperfect beings, we cannot be perfectly obedient—nor does God expect us to be. What He does want and deserve, however, is our sincere desire to please Him and to follow Him.

Are you willing to conform your behavior to God's rules? If you can answer that question with a resounding yes, God will use you and bless you—today, tomorrow, and every day of your life.

*Obedience is a foundational
stepping-stone on the path of God's Will.*
Elizabeth George

Finding Inspiration at Church

We are God's fellow workers; you are
God's field, you are God's building.

1 CORINTHIANS 3:9 NKJV

Your church isn't just a place to find God. It's also a place to find inspiration, fellowship, purpose, and comfort.

The church belongs to God; it is His just as certainly as we are His. When we help build God's church—the body of Christ—we bear witness to the changes He has made in our lives.

Today and every day, let us worship God with grateful hearts and helping hands as we support the church He has created. Let us share our faith with our friends, our families, and the world. When we do, we'll bless others—and we'll be blessed by the One who sent His Son to bring transformation to our lives and our world.

Make your church grow: some assembly required.
Church sign

Your Future in His Hands

*I know the thoughts that I think toward you, says
the Lord, thoughts of peace and not of evil, to give
you a future and a hope. Then you will call upon Me
and go and pray to Me, and I will listen to you.*

JEREMIAH 29:11–12 NKJV

Here are a few questions worth pondering: Are you willing to place your future in the hands of a loving and all-knowing God? Do you trust in the ultimate goodness of His plan for your life? And will you face today's challenges with optimism and hope? If you answered each of these questions with a resounding yes, congratulations are in order. After all, God created you for a very important reason: His reason. And you have important work to do: His work.

So today, as you live in the present and look to the future, remember that God has a very important plan for you. And while you still have time, it's up to you to act—and to believe—accordingly.

*Do not limit the limitless God! With Him,
face the future unafraid because you are never alone.*
Lettie Cowman

Ask and Receive

*Ask, and it will be given to you; seek, and you
will find; knock, and it will be opened to you. For
everyone who asks receives, and he who seeks finds,
and to him who knocks it will be opened.*

MATTHEW 7:7–8 NKJV

Jesus told His disciples that they should petition God to meet their needs. But His instruction wasn't just for them—it's for us, too. Genuine, heartfelt prayer brings powerful changes in us and in our world. When we lift our hearts to God, we open ourselves to a never-ending source of divine wisdom and infinite love.

Do you have questions about your future? Do you have needs that you simply can't meet by yourself? Do you need comfort? If so, talk to God about it. Ask Him for direction and provision, and to soothe the ache in your heart; keep asking Him for what you need, every day that you live. Whatever you face, pray about it—and never lose hope. God is listening, and He's perfectly capable of answering your prayers. But it's up to you to ask.

*God's help is near and always available, but
it is only given to those who seek it.*
Max Lucado

He'll Be There for You

God, who got you started in this spiritual adventure,
shares with us the life of his Son and our
Master Jesus. He will never give up on you.

1 CORINTHIANS 1:9 MSG

Sometimes the way forward seems impossible to divine, and the future seems dark and murky instead of bright and clear. These are the moments we have to lean on God the most.

Sooner or later, we all confront circumstances that trouble us, even shake us to the core of our souls. That's precisely the moment we need God's comfort—and He will be there for us. So the next time you find your courage stretched to the limit, lean on God's promises. He'll walk with you through life's adventure and He'll never give up on you.

*As sure as God puts his children in the furnace
he will be in the furnace with them.*

C. H. Spurgeon

Priorities . . . Moment by Moment

*You can't go wrong when you love others. When you add
up everything in the law code, the sum total is love. But
make sure that you don't get so absorbed and exhausted
in taking care of all your day-by-day obligations that you
lose track of the time and doze off, oblivious to God.*

ROMANS 13:10–11 MSG

Each waking moment holds the potential for you to think
a creative thought or offer a heartfelt prayer. So even if
you're a person with too many demands and too few hours in
which to meet them, take comfort in the knowledge that when
you sincerely seek to discover God's priorities for your life, He
will provide answers in marvelous and surprising ways.

This is the day God has made, and He has filled it with
opportunities to love, to serve, and to seek His guidance. Seize
those opportunities. And as a gift to yourself, to your family,
and to the world, slow down and take each day moment by
moment. You'll soon discover that God's blessings come
tucked in the pockets of right priorities.

Putting first things first is an issue at the very heart of life.
Stephen Covey

A Walk with God

*Set an example of good works yourself, with
integrity and dignity in your teaching.*

TITUS 2:7 HCSB

It has been said that character is what we are when nobody is watching. If we sincerely wish to walk with God, we must strive, to the best of our abilities, to follow God's path and to obey His instructions—even when we think no one's looking. In short, we must recognize the importance integrity should play in our lives.

When we listen carefully to God's voice in our hearts, and when we behave in ways that are consistent with His leading, we can't help but receive His blessing.

So today and every day, listen carefully to the Spirit's voice. Build your life on the firm foundation of integrity. When you do, you won't need to look over your shoulder to see who, besides God, is watching.

*In matters of style, swim with the current;
In matters of principle, stand like a rock.*
Thomas Jefferson

The Gift of Cheerfulness

Worry is a heavy load, but a kind word cheers you up.

PROVERBS 12:25 NCV

God promises us lives of joy if we accept His love and His grace and follow His ways. Yet sometimes, even the most righteous fall into the pits of ill temper and frustration. During these moments, we may not feel like turning our thoughts and prayers heavenward, but that's precisely what we must do. Only then can our Helper lighten our load and our hearts. When we commune with our heavenly Father, we simply can't stay grumpy for long. Instead, we'll be able to go out and share a cheerful word with some other heavy heart.

Accept God's gift of cheerfulness, and share it with someone today.

And so of cheerfulness . . . the more it is spent, the more of it remains.
Ralph Waldo Emerson

Comforting Others

A word spoken at the right time is like
golden apples on a silver tray.

PROVERBS 25:11 HCSB

When you meet others in need, offer comfort by sharing your courage, your help, and your faith. As the renowned revivalist Vance Havner observed, "No journey is complete that does not lead through some dark valleys. We can properly comfort others only with the comfort wherewith we ourselves have been comforted of God."

Are you in need of comfort today? Discover the miracle of healing that comes when you reach out to comfort others.

Discouraged people don't need critics. They hurt enough already. They don't need more guilt or piled-on distress. They need encouragement. They need a refuge, a willing, caring, available someone.
Charles Swindoll

Dream Big

A dream fulfilled is a tree of life.

PROVERBS 13:12 NLT

Sometimes it's easier to dream than it is to believe in those dreams. We may have high hopes and big plans, but when the storm clouds of life form overhead, it's tempting to give up. Tempting, but potentially tragic. After all, with God as our partner, no challenge is too great, and no mountain is too high.

If you've encountered a setback or two, don't worry too much about your troubles—and never abandon your hopes. Instead, focus on your dreams. They do come true, especially to those who take steps toward achieving them.

*The future belongs to those who believe
in the beauty of their dreams.*
Eleanor Roosevelt

Specific Prayers

God answered their prayers because they trusted Him.

1 Chronicles 5:20 MSG

As the old saying goes, if it's big enough to worry about, it's big enough to pray about. Yet sometimes we don't pray about the specific details of our lives. Instead, we may offer general prayers that are decidedly heavy on platitudes and decidedly light on particulars.

The next time you pray, try this: be very specific about the things you ask God to do. Of course God already knows precisely what you need—He knows infinitely more about your life than you do—but you need the experience of talking to your Creator in honest, unambiguous language.

So today don't be vague with God. Tell Him exactly what you need. He doesn't need to hear the details, but you do.

There will be no power in our lives apart from prayer.
Angela Thomas

Discipline Yourself

Discipline yourself for the purpose of godliness.

1 TIMOTHY 4:7 NASB

Your disciplined approach to life can help you build a more meaningful relationship with God. How can that be? Because God expects all of His followers to lead lives of disciplined obedience to Him . . . and He rewards those who do.

Sometimes it's hard to be disciplined. But persevere: self-discipline never goes out of style.

Your greatest accomplishments in life will probably require plenty of work and a heaping helping of self-discipline—which, by the way, is in line with God's plan. After all, He has promised to give you the strength and to walk with you all along the way. He has big plans for you, and He'll do His part to fulfill those plans. Will you do yours?

 If one examines the secret behind a championship football team, a magnificent orchestra, or a successful business, the principal ingredient is invariably discipline.

James Dobson

The Opportunity to Serve

The one who blesses others is abundantly
blessed; those who help others are helped.

PROVERBS 11:25 MSG

Here's a question for you: Will you consider each day another opportunity to celebrate life and improve your little corner of the world? Hopefully so, because your corner of the world, like so many others, can use all the help it can get.

You can make a difference in the quality of your own life and the lives of your family, your neighbors, your friends, and your community. You make the world a better place whenever you find a need and fill it. And in these difficult days, the needs are great—but so are your abilities to meet those needs.

So as you plan for the day ahead, be sure to make time for service. Father's orders. And then expect God to richly reward your generosity.

There is nothing small in the service of God.
Saint Francis de Sales

Enthusiastic Service

Do your work with enthusiasm. Work as if you were serving the Lord, not as if you were serving only men and women.

EPHESIANS 6:7 NCV

This day, like every day, should be cause for celebration. After all, God is good, and His blessings are too numerous to count. In response to the Creator's gifts, we are wise to serve Him with fervor and enthusiasm.

Do you see each day as a glorious opportunity to serve God and to do His will? Are you excited about God's gifts and your own future? Or do you struggle through each day giving scarcely a thought to His blessings?

You are the recipient of Christ's sacrificial love. Accept it enthusiastically and share it freely. God deserves your enthusiasm; the world needs it, and you'll be blessed by the experience of sharing it.

Each day I look for a kernel of excitement.
Barbara Jordan

Judging Others

*There is only one Lawgiver and Judge, the one
who is able to save and destroy. But you—
who are you to judge your neighbor?*

JAMES 4:12 NIV

Okay, answer honestly: do you find it easy to judge others? If so, you're not alone; we humans are often quick, too quick, in fact, to judge others. Yet in our better moments, we should remember that, in matters of judgment, God does not need (or want) our help in judging. Why? Because God is perfectly capable of judging the human heart . . . while we are not.

All of us have fallen short of God's laws, and none of us, therefore, is qualified to "cast the first stone." Thankfully, God has forgiven us, and we, too, must forgive others. Let us refrain, then, from judging our family members, our friends, and our loved ones. Instead, let us forgive them and love them in the same way that God has forgiven us and loves us.

*Here's a simple rule of thumb:
Don't judge other people more harshly
than you want God to judge you.*
Marie T. Freeman

Transformation

His message was simple and austere, like his desert surroundings: "Change your life. God's kingdom is here."
MATTHEW 3:2 MSG

God has the power to transform your life and the lives of your loved ones. And as a thoughtful person, it's your job to ask Him to do it.

God stands at the door and waits; all you must do is knock. When you do, God always answers.

So today and every day, be sure to take every step of your journey with God as your companion. Study His Word, follow His instructions, talk to Him often, and honor His Son. And while you're at it, be an example of the genuine difference that God can make in the lives of people (like you) who trust Him completely. When you do, you'll be transformed, and you'll be blessed . . . now and forever.

God's work is not in buildings, but in transformed lives.
Ruth Bell Graham

Being Comfortable with Your Finances

Trust in your money and down you go!
But the godly flourish like leaves in spring.

PROVERBS 11:28 NLT

From time to time, most of us struggle with money—both how to get it and how to spend it. Sometimes our financial struggles are simply manifestations of the inner conflict we feel when we stray from God's plan.

God doesn't intend for us to keep acquiring more and more stuff. Instead, His Word teaches us to be levelheaded, moderate, and thoughtful about the way we spend the money He entrusts to us. Today, promise that you'll do whatever it takes to create a sensible financial plan and stick to it. Know where your money is coming from and where it's going. When you become comfortable with your finances, you'll become more comfortable with every other aspect of your life.

That man is rich whose pleasures are cheapest.
Henry David Thoreau

Faith and Wholeness

The just shall live by faith.

HEBREWS 10:38 NKJV

In the ninth chapter of Matthew, we are told of a suffering woman who sought healing in a dramatic way: she simply touched the hem of Jesus's garment. When she did, Christ turned and said, "Daughter, be of good comfort; thy faith hath made thee whole" (Matthew 9:22 KJV). We, too, can be made whole when we place our faith completely and unwaveringly in God.

As you learn to trust God more and more, you'll be amazed at the marvelous things He can do with you and through you. So strengthen your faith through praise, through worship, through Bible study, and through prayer. Then, trust God's plans. Your Heavenly Father is waiting for you. If you reach out to Him in faith, He will give you peace and heal your broken spirit. Be content to touch even the smallest fragment of the Master's garment, and He will make you whole.

God loves us the way we are, but He loves us too much to leave us that way.
Leighton Ford

The Thread of Generosity

Freely you have received, freely give.

MATTHEW 10:8 NIV

I t's not complicated: input determines output. What you sow determines what you'll reap. So if you want to enjoy a generous life, sow seeds of generosity.

The thread of generosity is woven into the fabric of Christ's teachings. As He sent His disciples out to heal the sick and spread God's message of salvation, Jesus offered this guiding principle: "Freely you have received, freely give." That principle still applies.

So if you'd like to experience more of God's abundance, try sharing more of it. Generosity isn't restricted to material things, either. Do you seek God's comfort and His peace? Then comfort those around you. Share your possessions, yes. But also share your faith and your love. When you plant the seeds of generosity in others, you'll find you reap an even more bountiful harvest in return.

Abundant living means abundant giving.
E. Stanley Jones

His Comforting Hand

God, who comforts the downcast, comforted us.

2 CORINTHIANS 7:6 NIV

God comforts all who reach out to Him. When we're feeling discouraged, worried, lonely, or afraid, we can call on our heavenly Father in prayer and He will respond to our concerns.

Sometimes God responds by filling our spirits with a sense of peace, a calm that only He can provide. Sometimes He uses our friends and family members to comfort us. And sometimes God performs miracles in our lives, transforming our defeats into victories and our failures into triumphs.

God's response to our needs is varied, but we need never doubt that He will respond in the way He knows is best. When we reach out to God, He reaches back with His comforting hand. When we ask, He answers. He knows our needs, and He knows how best to provide for us. We need only ask, trust, and accept His comfort and His love.

Put your hand into the hand of God.
He gives the calmness and serenity of heart and soul.
Lettie B. Cowman

Today's Opportunities to Encourage

*Encourage each other daily, while it is still called today,
so that none of you is hardened by sin's deception.*

HEBREWS 3:13 HCSB

E ach day brings opportunities to encourage others and to commend their good works. When we do, we spread seeds of joy and happiness.

God grants each of us the gift of life, and He asks us to celebrate it. One important part of each day's celebration is the time we spend celebrating others: by honoring their accomplishments, rejoicing in their victories, and recognizing their efforts. But it doesn't stop there. People also need our unconditional encouragement—heartening words regardless of whether they've been successful in their efforts today. They need encouragement simply regarding who they are, not what they've done.

Today, be slow to criticize and quick to encourage. When you do, you'll be a powerful force for good in the world . . . and for God.

*If someone listens or stretches out a hand or whispers
a word of encouragement or attempts to understand a
lonely person, extraordinary things begin to happen.*

Loretta Girzaitis

Expecting the Best

*This is the day the Lord has made; let
us rejoice and be glad in it.*

PSALM 118:24 NIV

What do you expect from the day ahead? Are you anticipating the wonderful things God will do, or are you living under a cloud of apprehension and doubt? The familiar words of Psalm 118:24 remind us that each day should be a cause for celebration. After all, God blesses us abundantly every day of our lives. He gives us love and assurance. He gives us comfort when we're hurting. And, most importantly, God promises us the priceless gift of eternal life. As we consider these blessings, our hearts can rejoice and be truly glad.

Daily life brings many challenges. But when we arm ourselves with the promises of God's Word, we can expect the best—not only for the day ahead, but for all eternity.

*Each day, each moment is so pregnant with eternity
that if we tune in to it, we can hardly contain the joy.*
Gloria Gaither

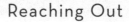

Reaching Out

Don't be obsessed with getting your own advantage.
Forget yourselves long enough to lend a helping hand.

PHILIPPIANS 2:4 MSG

Noted American theologian Phillips Brooks once advised, "Be such a man, and live such a life, that if every man were such as you, and every life a life like yours, this earth would be God's Paradise."

Sometimes, when we feel happy or generous, we find it easy to do good. Other times, when we're discouraged or weary, we can scarcely summon the energy to utter a single kind word. But the instruction in God's Word is clear: we are to think of others and help them rather than always focusing on our own wants and needs.

Today, consider all the things God has done for you. Forget for a moment about what you want, and reach out to help someone in need. You'll find it brings an even better reward than when you're only looking out for yourself.

It is one of the most beautiful compensations of life
that no man can sincerely try to help
another without helping himself.
Ralph Waldo Emerson

Love Thy Neighbor

Each one of us needs to look after the good of
the people around us, asking ourselves, "How
can I help?" That's exactly what Jesus did.

ROMANS 15:2–3 MSG

This very day, you will encounter someone who needs a word of comfort, a pat on the back, a helping hand, or a heartfelt prayer. And in the rush and press of your busy day, it's easy to say you don't have time. But stop for just a moment and consider this: If you don't reach out to this person, who will? If you don't take the time to understand the needs of your neighbors, who will?

Today, pay attention to other people's needs and struggles, and find a way—however small—to lift them up.

*The purpose of human life is to serve, and to show
compassion and the will to help others.*
Albert Schweitzer

OCTOBER

Honesty with Yourself

> Good people will be guided by honesty.
>
> PROVERBS 11:3 NCV

Honesty is important, and that includes being honest with ourselves. But because we view the world through the subjective lenses of our own particular attitudes and beliefs, it's often hard to be objective about our behaviors, our strengths, our weaknesses, and our motivations.

Do you take the time to honestly assess yourself—to analyze the way you typically think and behave? Honest self-evaluation is the foundation of lasting self-improvement. And it can help you become more comfortable with who you are and who you want to become. So don't be afraid to look in the mirror and be honest about (and with) the person you see there. Don't be too hard on yourself, but do look for ways to improve . . . and then get started. The person in the mirror will be glad you did.

It isn't until you come to a spiritual understanding of who you are . . . that you can begin to take control.
Oprah Winfrey

Laugh!

A happy heart makes the face cheerful.

Proverbs 15:13 niv

Laughter is God's gift, and He intends for us to enjoy it. Yet sometimes, because of the inevitable stresses of everyday life, laughter seems like a distant memory.

We have every reason to be cheerful and to be thankful. Our blessings from God are beyond measure. So why do we trudge through life with frowns on our faces and sighs in our hearts? Few things in life are more displeasing than the sight of a man or woman grumpily complaining about everything in sight. And few things are more uplifting than the sight of a cheerful man or woman smiling and laughing through life.

Today, as you go about your daily activities, approach life with a grin and a chuckle. After all, God created laughter for our happiness . . . so laugh!

Laughter is an instant vacation!
Milton Berle

Mentors That Matter

The lips of the righteous feed many.

PROVERBS 10:21 HCSB

Here's a simple yet effective way to improve your life: choose role models whom you admire, and do your best to follow the good examples they set. When you do, you'll become a stronger person as you grow spiritually and emotionally.

Today, as a gift to yourself, select a godly mentor whose judgment you trust. Then listen carefully to his or her advice—and be willing to accept that advice, even if following it requires effort or even some discomfort.

Whether we're nineteen or ninety-five, we still have lots to learn—and a mentor can help us learn it. Consider your mentor one of God's gifts to you. Thank Him for that gift, and invest in the relationship for His glory.

Do not open your heart to every man, but discuss your affairs with one who is wise and who fears God.

Thomas à Kempis

Blessed Obedience

When you and your children return to the Lord your God and
obey him with all your heart and with all your soul according
to everything I command you today, then the Lord your God
will restore your fortunes and have compassion on you and
gather you again from all the nations where he scattered you.

DEUTERONOMY 30:2–3 NIV

We live in a world filled with temptations, distractions,
and countless opportunities to wander far from the path
God has laid out for us. But as men and women who seek to be
positive role models for our families, we must turn our thoughts
and our hearts away from the temptations and distractions
around us. We must turn instead to God, seeking His counsel
often—and trusting and following the counsel He gives.

When we invite God to rule over our hearts and our lives,
our obedience will bring with it blessing. So today and every
day, vow to live according to God's rules, not the world's rules.
The world may lead you astray, but God never will. You're safe
with Him.

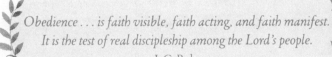

Obedience . . . is faith visible, faith acting, and faith manifest.
It is the test of real discipleship among the Lord's people.
J. C. Ryle

Never Give In

We are hard-pressed on every side, yet not
crushed; we are perplexed, but not in despair.

2 Corinthians 4:8 NKJV

A well-lived life calls for preparation, determination, and lots of perseverance. For an example of perfect perseverance, we need look no further than the life of Jesus. The carpenter from Nazareth finished what He started.

Despite His suffering, and despite the shame of the cross, Jesus was steadfast in His faithfulness to God. He never gave up and He never gave in. We, too, must remain faithful, especially during times of hardship. Sometimes it seems our prayers are met only with silence; yet even then we must patiently persevere, knowing that God is indeed listening and working on our behalf.

Are you facing a tough situation? A perplexing dilemma? A heartbreaking disappointment? If so, remember this: never give in; whatever your problem, God is willing and able to see you through.

Never give in, never give in, never, never, never, never—
in nothing, great or small, large or petty—never give
in except to convictions of honour and good sense.
Winston Churchill

The Capacity to Forgive

Smart people know how to hold their tongue;
their grandeur is to forgive and forget.

PROVERBS 19:11 MSG

Martin Luther King Jr. became a symbol of strength and dignity for African Americans during the turbulent 1960s. And as an acknowledgment of his role in the fight for freedom and justice, he received the Nobel Peace Prize in 1964.

It was King who said, "We must develop and maintain the capacity to forgive." This is great advice, but forgiveness can be easier said than done. Sometimes we have to work at it for years, trying to forgive those who have hurt us while trying to make peace with the past.

Forgiveness is seldom easy, but it's always worthwhile. We're closer to our Creator when we turn the other cheek, while continuing to stand up for what is right.

One of the most time-consuming things is to have an enemy.
E. B. White

The Miracle Worker

> You are the God who performs miracles; you
> display your power among the peoples.
>
> PSALM 77:14 NIV

G od is a miracle worker. Throughout history, He has intervened in the course of human events in ways that cannot be explained by science or by human rationale. And He's still doing so today.

God's miracles are not limited to special occasions, nor are they witnessed only by a select few. God displays His wonders all around us: the miracle of a newborn baby; the miracle of a world renewing itself with every sunrise; the miracle of lives transformed by God's love and grace. Each day, God's handiwork is evident for all to see and experience.

Today, seize the opportunity to see God's hand at work. His miracles come in a variety of shapes and sizes, so keep your eyes and your heart open. Be watchful, and you'll soon be amazed.

Too many times we miss so much because we live on the low level of the natural, the ordinary, the explainable.

Vance Havner

A Passionate Life

Never be lacking in zeal, but keep your
spiritual fervor, serving the Lord.

ROMANS 12:11 NIV

Are you passionate about your life, your loved ones, your work, and your faith? If you're a person who trusts God's promises, you have even more of an excuse to be passionate. After all, God's Word tells us we have every reason to be enthusiastic about life here on earth—and the life hereafter. But sometimes the messy struggles of life can leave us feeling decidedly unenthusiastic.

If you feel that your passion for life is slowly fading away, maybe now's the time to slow down, to rest, to count your blessings, and to pray. When you feel worried or weary, fervently petition God to renew your sense of wonder and excitement.

Life with God is a glorious adventure; revel in it. As long as you're alive, live passionately.

Heat is required to forge anything.
Every great accomplishment is the story of a flaming heart.
Arthur H. Glascow

He Renews Us

I will give you a new heart and put a new spirit within you.

<small>EZEKIEL 36:26 HCSB</small>

God intends for us to lead joyous lives filled with abundance and peace. But sometimes, as all of us can attest, abundance and peace seem very far away. It is then that we must turn to God for renewal. When we do, He will restore us.

Have you tapped in to the power of God, or are you muddling along under your own power? If you are weary, worried, fretful, or fearful, then it is time to turn to a strength much greater than your own.

The Bible promises that with God all things are possible. Are you ready to turn things over to Him? If you do, you'll soon discover that the Creator of the universe stands ready and able to create a new sense of wonderment and joy in you.

Sometimes, we need a housecleaning of the heart.
Catherine Marshall

Church Matters

*I was glad when they said to me, "Let us
go to the house of the Lord."*

PSALM 122:1 NLT

The Bible teaches that we should worship God in our
hearts and in community with other believers. We have
clear instructions to "feed the church of God" (where "church"
equals "people") and to worship our Creator in the presence
of others.

Yet it's not always easy to find the time to become actively
involved in a church.

We live in a world that is teeming with temptations and
distractions. Our challenge, of course, is to ensure that we rise
above the challenges of everyday life. We do so when we make
God the central focus of our lives. One way that we remain
faithful to the Creator is through the practice of regular, purposeful worship with our families. When we worship the
Father faithfully, fervently, and frequently, we are blessed.

*Our churches are meant to be havens where
the caste rules of the world do not apply.*
Beth Moore

Patience Pays

Patience is better than pride.
ECCLESIASTES 7:8 NLT

The rigors of childcare can test the patience of the most mild-mannered men and women. After all, even the best-behaved children may, on occasion, do things that worry us or confuse us or anger us. Why? Because they are children and because they are human.

We must be patient with the shortcomings of the kids in our lives (just as they, too, must be patient with ours). Why? Because sometimes, patience is the price we pay for being responsible adults.

So today, do yourself and your loved ones this favor: be patient with everybody, starting with the person you see when you look in the mirror. And while you're at it, be sure to be equally patient with all those folks you see when you look through your family photo album.

Waiting is an essential part of spiritual discipline.
It can be the ultimate test of faith.
Anne Graham Lotz

Doers of the Word

Prove yourselves doers of the word, and not merely hearers.

JAMES 1:22 NASB

The old saying is both familiar and true: actions speak louder than words. So our actions should always give testimony to the positive changes God can make in the lives of those who walk with Him.

God calls upon each of us to act in accordance with His will and with respect for His commandments. If we are to be faithful followers of our heavenly Father, we must realize that it's never enough simply to hear His instructions; we must also live by them. And it is never enough to wait idly by while others do good works; we, too, must act. Doing God's work is a responsibility each of us must bear. But when we do, our loving heavenly Father will reward our efforts with a bountiful harvest.

[He] who wait[s] until circumstances completely favor his undertaking will never accomplish anything.
Martin Luther

The Abundant Life

I came that they may have life, and have it abundantly.
JOHN 10:10 NASB

In John 10:10, the Bible gives us hope—we are told that abundance and contentment can be ours. But what, exactly, did Jesus mean when He promised abundant life? Was He referring to material possessions or financial wealth? No. He was talking about something more important and more lasting. Jesus was describing a different kind of abundance: a spiritual richness that extends beyond the temporal boundaries of this world.

Is material abundance part of God's plan for our lives? Not necessarily. In every circumstance of life, whether in times of wealth or times of want, God will provide us with whatever we need if we trust Him. May we, as children of God, accept His abundance with open arms and open hearts. And may we share His blessings with all who cross our paths.

*God will either give us what we ask, or
what He knows to be better for us.*
Bernard of Clairvaux

One Mouth, Two Ears, Lots of Encouragement

Everyone should be quick to listen, slow to speak and slow to become angry, for man's anger does not bring about the righteous life that God desires.

JAMES 1:19–20 NIV

God's Word instructs us to be quick to listen and slow to speak. And when it comes to the important job of encouraging our friends and family members, we're wise to listen carefully (first) and then offer helpful words (second).

Perhaps God gave us two ears and one mouth for a reason— so that we might listen twice as much as we speak. After all, listening quietly to another person can sometimes be a wonderful form of encouragement. Besides, after you've listened carefully to the other person, you're more likely to speak wisely.

Today and every day, you have the power to comfort others with your words *and* your ears . . . with an emphasis on the latter. Sometimes the words you *don't* speak are just as comforting as the ones you *do*.

The battle of the tongue is won not in the mouth, but in the heart.
Annie Chapman

OCTOBER 15

Looking Forward with Hope

If we look forward to something we don't yet have,
we must wait patiently and confidently.

ROMANS 8:25 NLT

At a college track meet, one young man set three world records in under an hour. As an Olympian, he humiliated Adolf Hitler by winning four gold medals in the 1936 Summer Olympics in Berlin. The man was Jesse Owens—grandson of slaves, son of an Alabama sharecropper, and one of the greatest athletes of the twentieth century.

Owens was, by nature, an optimist. He said, "Find the good. It's all around you. Find it, showcase it, and you'll start believing in it."

The next time you find yourself caught up in the rat race, remember Jesse Owens. Look for the good, expect the best, and set about pursuing your dreams. When you look through eyes of hope, you can look forward with confidence.

Never yield to gloomy anticipation.
Place your hope and confidence in God.
He has no record of failure.
Lettie B. Cowman

What Doesn't Change

Unfailing love surrounds those who trust the Lord.

PSALM 32:10 NLT

Every day we encounter a multitude of changes—some good, some not so good, and some downright disheartening. On those occasions when we must endure devastating personal losses that leave us stunned and seemingly unable to move, we can turn to God for comfort and assurance. When we do, our loving heavenly Father stands ready to protect us, to comfort us, to guide us, and, in time, to heal us.

Are you facing an unwelcome change or life-altering setback? If so, don't suffer alone. Run to God for the ultimate source of comfort. He never changes . . . and He will surround you with His unfailing love.

God carries your picture in His wallet.
Tony Campolo

A Wing and a Prayer

Be cheerful. Keep things in good repair. Keep your spirits
up. Think in harmony. Be agreeable. Do all that, and
the God of love and peace will be with you for sure.

2 CORINTHIANS 13:11 MSG

We should never underestimate the power of a kind word, a sincere smile, a pat on the back, or a heartfelt hug. And we must never underestimate the importance of cheerfulness. The Bible teaches us that a cheerful heart is like medicine: it makes us (and the people around us) feel better.

Cheerfulness begins on the inside—in our hearts, our thoughts, and our prayers—and works its way out from there.

The world would like you to think that material possessions can bring happiness, but don't believe it. Lasting happiness can't be bought; it's the result of diligent effort in the disciplines of positive thought, heartfelt prayer, and good deeds. But a cheerful heart blessed by God's love and peace is well worth the effort.

Wondrous is the strength of cheerfulness.
Thomas Carlyle

God Is Here

Draw near to God, and He will draw near to you.

JAMES 4:8 HCSB

God is constantly making Himself available to us. So when we approach Him sincerely—with our hearts and minds lifted up to Him in prayer—we can sense His presence and His love. Why, then, does the Creator sometimes seem distant from us . . . or altogether absent? The answer has little to do with God and everything to do with us. When God seems far removed from our lives, it's a result of our own emotional struggles and shortcomings, not an indication of God's absence.

We all have times when we feel far from God. Even though it's usually because we've put the distance between us and Him, that's actually good news. Because anytime we genuinely desire to establish a closer relationship with the Creator, we can do so—all we have to do is draw near to Him. When you do that, He will be right by your side . . . always.

[God] always shows up. He always saves. He always rescues. His timing is not ours. His methods are usually unconventional. But what we can know, what we can settle in our soul, is that He is faithful to come when we call.

Angela Thomas

Keep Swinging

*In my distress I prayed to the Lord, and the Lord answered me
and set me free. The Lord is for me, so I will have no fear.*

Psalm 118:5–6 nlt

Babe Ruth overcame a troubled childhood to become, perhaps, the greatest figure in the history of baseball. His philosophy at the plate mirrored his outlook on life: swing away,
and give it all you've got. So it's no coincidence that the Babe
achieved records for both home runs and strikeouts.

Ruth once advised, "Never let the fear of striking out get
in your way." And that's smart play on the diamond or off. So
the next time you're facing a tough pitch, think of a poor boy
who grew up on the wrong side of the tracks, but kept swinging
until he slugged his way into the Hall of Fame. And don't
worry about a few strikeouts, because there's always another at
bat for people who simply won't stop swinging.

Only those who dare to fail greatly can ever achieve greatly.
Robert Kennedy

Diligence Matters

Buy the truth and do not sell it; get wisdom,
discipline and understanding.

PROVERBS 23:23 NIV

God's Word makes it clear: we are instructed to be disciplined, diligent, moderate, and mature. But the world often tempts us to behave in other ways. Everywhere we turn, or so it seems, we are faced with powerful incentives to behave in ways that are undisciplined, immoderate, and imprudent.

You know God rewards diligence and righteousness. And you know that God often teaches His lessons sooner rather than later. So practice the fine art of self-discipline . . . and just as important, practice it now.

*If your determination is fixed, I do not counsel you to despair.
Few things are impossible to diligence and skill. Great
works are performed not by strength, but perseverance.*
Samuel Johnson

Secure in His Love

The faithful love of the Lord never ends!

LAMENTATIONS 3:22 NLT

We live in a time of uncertainty and danger, a time when even the most courageous among us have legitimate cause for concern. But we can find comfort in the knowledge that God loves us, that He will guide us, and that He will protect us. When we think carefully and prayerfully about the role God can (and should) play in our lives, we can live courageously, knowing that we are secure in our Father's love.

Cast your anxieties unto the Lord. Seek protection from the Almighty. And then live courageously, knowing that even in these troubled times you need not fear.

*A man who is intimate with God
will never be intimidated by men.*
Leonard Ravenhill

Dealing with Disappointment

*We were burdened beyond measure, above strength,
so that we despaired even of life. Yes, we had the
sentence of death in ourselves, that we should not
trust in ourselves but in God who raises the dead, who
delivered us from so great a death, and does deliver
us; in whom we trust that He will still deliver us.*

2 CORINTHIANS 1:8–10 NKJV

From time to time, each of us must endure trouble and disappointments that leave us scratching our heads wondering, "Why me?" Often these events come unexpectedly, leaving us with too many questions and not enough answers. Yet even when we don't have all the answers—or, for that matter, when we don't seem to have any of the answers—God does. And since our Creator loves us without condition, we need never give up or give in.

Whatever your circumstances, whether you're standing atop the highest mountain or wandering through the darkest valley, God is with you and will comfort you when you go to him in faith. When you are burdened, He will carry it for you.

One's best successes come after disappointments.
Henry Ward Beecher

Having Faith

Lord, I believe; help my unbelief!

MARK 9:24 NKJV

Even the most faithful men and women can be overcome by occasional bouts of fear and doubt. When these begin to grow, what should you do? The answer is straightforward: whenever you feel that your faith is being tested or pushed to its limits, seek the comfort, the assurance, and the love of your heavenly Father.

Even if you feel distant from God, you can be certain that He is never distant from you. To the contrary, He is always with you, always ready to reassure you if you reach out to Him. When you sincerely seek God's presence, He will comfort your heart, calm your fears, and restore your faith in the future . . . and your faith in Him.

We basically have two choices to make in dealing with the mysteries of God. We can wrestle with Him or we can rest in Him.
Calvin Miller

Blessing Others

Be agreeable, be sympathetic, be loving, be
compassionate, be humble. That goes for all of you,
no exceptions. No retaliation. No sharp-tongued
sarcasm. Instead, bless—that's your job, to bless.

1 PETER 3:8–9 MSG

As a thoughtful person who's been richly blessed by the Creator, you have every reason to be optimistic about life—and you have every reason to share your hope with others.

Make no mistake: one of the reasons God placed you here on earth is so that you might become a beacon of His light and an encouragement to the world. When you give hope to others, before long they give it to others still . . . and eventually it comes back to you.

As you go about your tasks today, celebrate the good that you find in others. And strive to bring light into the lives of everyone you meet.

*There are no words to express the abyss between
isolation and having one ally. It may be conceded to
the mathematician that four is twice two. But two is
not twice one; two is two thousand times one.*

G. K. Chesterton

Striving for Significance

*The Lord directs the steps of the godly. He delights in
every detail of their lives. Though they stumble, they
will never fall, for the Lord holds them by the hand.*

PSALM 37:23–24 NLT

Sometimes it's easy to look at famous people and presume
that their lives have more significance than our own. But
if we assume, even for a moment, that our own lives are less
important, we are mistaken. God has a plan for each of us, a
direction in which He is leading us, a path of great significance
to Him. Our task, simply stated, is to discover, as best we can,
what God wants us to do . . . and to do it.

It's comforting to know that when we're following God's
path, our lives have ultimate—and eternal—meaning. Novelist Willa Cather observed, "Life [hurries] past us . . . , too
strong to stop, too sweet to lose." Life indeed hurries, but remember that no matter what stage of life you're in, there is still
time to do significant work . . . work that no one but you can
do. And the best day to begin that work is today.

*It's incredible to realize that what we do each day
has meaning in the big picture of God's plan.*
Bill Hybels

Choices

*Cheerfully pleasing God is the main thing, and that's
what we aim to do, regardless of our conditions.*

2 CORINTHIANS 5:9 MSG

From the instant you wake up in the morning until the moment you nod off to sleep at night, you make lots of decisions: decisions about the things you do, decisions about the words you speak, and decisions about the thoughts you choose to entertain. Simply put, your life is a series of choices—and the choices you make determine the direction and quality of your life.

If you sincerely want to lead a life that is pleasing to your Creator, make daily, moment-by-moment choices that are pleasing to Him. Think carefully—and prayerfully—about your choices. And when in doubt, don't make a move until you've talked things over with God.

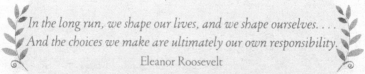

*In the long run, we shape our lives, and we shape ourselves. . . .
And the choices we make are ultimately our own responsibility.*
Eleanor Roosevelt

Unfulfilled Promises

*If you belonged to the world, its people would
love you. But you don't belong to the world. I
have chosen you to leave the world behind.*

<small>JOHN 15:19 CEV</small>

The world promises happiness, contentment, love, and abundance. But these are promises it simply cannot fulfill. True love and lasting happiness are not results of worldly possessions; they're results of the relationship we choose to have with God. The world's promises are incomplete and illusory; God's promises are unfailing. But to see God's promises fulfilled in our lives, we have to be willing to leave the world behind.

If you've grown weary of the world's unfulfilled promises, tired of looking for love in all the wrong places, take heart. You were not made for the world, and the world will never love you like God does. You were made for close, fulfilling fellowship with Him. So build your life on the firm foundation of God's promises; nothing else even comes close.

*Too many Christians have geared their program to please,
to entertain, and to gain favor from this world.
We are concerned with how much, instead of
how little, like this age we can become.*
Billy Graham

How to Win Friends

*A friend loves you all the time, and a
brother helps in time of trouble.*

PROVERBS 17:17 NCV

His name remains synonymous with enthusiasm and salesmanship: Dale Carnegie, the author of the perennial best seller *How to Win Friends and Influence People*. For nearly a century, men and women from all walks of life have attended classes that he designed. These classes teach confidence, motivation, and relationship skills.

Carnegie had specific advice about friendship. He said, "You can make more friends in two months by becoming more interested in other people than you can in two years by trying to get people interested in you." So if you want to win friends and influence people, take it from the man who wrote the book. Get genuinely and sincerely interested in them, and pretty soon, they'll get interested in you.

A friend may well be reckoned the masterpiece of nature.
Ralph Waldo Emerson

Light for Today

Lord, You light my lamp; my God illuminates my darkness.
PSALM 18:28 HCSB

The path to spiritual maturity unfolds day by day. Each day offers the opportunity to worship God, to ignore God, or to rebel against God. When we worship Him with our prayers, our words, our thoughts, and our actions, we'll be blessed by the richness of our relationship with the Father.

In quiet moments when we open our hearts to God, the One who made us keeps remaking us. He gives us direction, perspective, wisdom, and courage.

When it comes to your faith, you won't be "fully grown" in this lifetime. Spiritual maturity is a lifelong journey, but we have the comfort of knowing that God will light the path, one day at a time. God still has important lessons He wants to teach you. Today, ask Him to light your way . . . and then follow where He leads.

Growing into spiritual maturity is becoming less self-conscious and more God-conscious.
Mark Batterson

Great Faithfulness

The Lord is faithful; He will strengthen and guard
you from the evil one. . . . May the Lord direct your
hearts to God's love and Christ's endurance.

2 THESSALONIANS 3:3–5 HCSB

Are you tired, discouraged, or fearful? Be comforted: God is with you. Are you confused? Listen to the quiet voice of your heavenly Father. Are you bitter? Talk with God and seek His healing. Are you celebrating a great victory? Thank God and praise Him: He is the Giver of all things good.

In whatever condition you find yourself, trust God and be comforted. He is faithful and He will watch over you and give you the strength you need for today.

God's faithfulness and grace make the impossible possible.
Sheila Walsh

Always with You

*You will show me the way of life, granting me the joy of
your presence and the pleasures of living with you forever.*

PSALM 16:11 NLT

D o you ever wonder if God is really there? You're not the
first person to think such thoughts. In fact, some of the
grandest heroes in the Bible had their doubts. But when questions arise and doubts begin to creep into your mind, remember
this: you can take those questions and doubts to God. They don't
threaten Him. He already knows your heart and your mind . . .
so why not go to Him and give Him the chance to give you the
answers and the faith you seek? He will give you the assurance
that He's not only out there—He's right here, with you.

Today, quiet yourself long enough to sense His presence.
God will comfort your heart and renew your spirit. He's always
with you, willing to show you the way and grant you the pleasures of living with Him forever.

*We are never more fulfilled than when our longing
for God is met by His presence in our lives.*
Billy Graham

NOVEMBER

Caring for Aging Parents

Let them first learn to do their duty to their own family and to repay their parents or grandparents. That pleases God.

1 TIMOTHY 5:4 NCV

If you're responsible, either directly or indirectly, for the care of aging parents, you already know that it can be a challenging job. But you also know that caring for your loved ones is not simply a duty; it is also a responsibility and a privilege.

Caring for an elderly adult requires a mixture of diplomacy, patience, insight, perseverance, gentleness, strength, compassion, wisdom, empathy, and, most of all, an endless supply of love.

Sometimes the job of caring for aging parents may seem like a thankless task, but it is not. Even if your parents don't fully appreciate your sacrifices, God does. And of this you may be certain: the Lord will find surprising ways to reward your faithfulness.

No matter how old they grow, some people never lose their beauty. They merely move it from their faces into their hearts.
Martin Buxbaum

God's Attentiveness

The eyes of the Lord range throughout the earth to show Himself strong for those whose hearts are completely His.

2 CHRONICLES 16:9 HCSB

God is not distant, and He is not disinterested. To the contrary, your heavenly Father is attentive to your needs. In fact, God knows precisely what you need and when you need it. But He still wants to talk with you, and as someone who loves Him, you should want to talk to Him, too.

Do you have questions that you simply can't answer? Ask for the guidance of your Creator. Do you sincerely seek the gift of everlasting love and eternal life? Accept God's gift of grace. Whatever your need, no matter how great or small, pray about it. Instead of waiting for mealtimes or bedtimes, pray always and never lose heart. And remember: God is here, and He's ready to talk with you now. So please don't make Him wait another moment.

I want the presence of God Himself, or I don't want anything at all to do with religion. . . . I want all that God has or I don't want any.

A. W. Tozer

Above and Beyond Our Circumstances

We take the good days from God—why not also the bad days?
JOB 2:10 MSG

We live in a world where expectations can be high and demands can be even higher.

If you become discouraged with the direction of your day—or of your life—turn your thoughts and prayers to your Father in heaven. Focus on His blessings, not on your hardships. Seek His will and follow it. Ask Him to give you strength and expect Him to work miracles. He is a God of possibility, not negativity. He will guide you through your difficulties . . . and beyond them.

The strengthening of faith comes from staying with it in the hour of trial. We should not shrink from tests of faith.
Catherine Marshall

Understanding the Power of Faith

Blessed are all they that put their trust in Him.

PSALM 2:12 KJV

Faith is the foundation upon which great lives are built. Faith is a gift we give ourselves, one that pays rich dividends in good times and hard times.

Faith, like a tender seedling, can be nurtured or neglected. When we nurture our faith through prayer, meditation, and worship, God blesses our lives and lifts our spirits. But when we fail to consult the Creator early and often, we do ourselves and our loved ones a disservice.

If your faith is being tested, reach out to your heavenly Father. With Him, all things are possible, and He stands ready to renew your strength whenever you're ready to ask. So ask. And keep asking. Today and every day.

Worry never robs tomorrow of its sorrow,
it only saps today of its joy.
Leo Buscaglia

Thy Will Be Done

"Father, if it is Your will, take this cup away from Me;
nevertheless not My will, but Yours, be done."

LUKE 22:42 NKJV

When Jesus went to the Mount of Olives, as described in Luke 22, He poured out His heart to God. Jesus knew of the agony that He was destined to endure, but He also knew that God's will must be done. We, like Jesus, may face trials that bring fear and trembling to the depths of our souls, but like Christ, we must seek God's will, not our own.

God has a plan for all our lives, but He will not force it on us. To the contrary, He only makes His plans clear to those who genuinely and humbly seek His will. As this day unfolds, let us seek God's will and obey His Word. When we entrust our lives to Him completely and without reservation, He gives us the courage to face any challenge . . . and the peace to live according to His will.

*You cannot continue doing things your way and
accomplish God's purposes in His ways. Your thinking
cannot come close to God's thoughts. For you
to do the will of God, you must adjust your life
to Him, His purposes, and His ways.*

Henry Blackaby

A Good Example

In everything set them an example by doing what is good.
TITUS 2:7 NIV

Stephen Covey, author of *The 7 Habits of Highly Effective People*, said: "You cannot not model. It's impossible. People will see your example, positive or negative, as a pattern for the way life is lived." He was right: all of us are role models, whether we intend to be or not.

Are you a person whose behavior serves as a positive role model for others? Are you kind to everyone you meet, no matter his or her station in life? If so, you're a powerful force for good in a world that desperately needs positive influences such as yours—and God will bless you for it.

A holy life will produce the deepest impression.
Lighthouses blow no horns; they only shine.
D. L. Moody

Watching Over Your Family

*Through your faith God is protecting you by
his power until you receive this salvation.*

1 PETER 1:5 NLT

These are difficult days for our world and for our loved ones. But the good news is that God is bigger than all of our problems. God loves us and protects us. In times of trouble, He comforts us; in times of sorrow, He dries our tears. When we are troubled or weak or sorrowful, God is always near, ready to help.

Are you concerned for the well-being of the people you love? You're not alone. We live in a world where temptations and dangers seem to lurk on every street corner. Parents and children alike have good reason to be watchful. But despite the challenges of our time, God remains steadfast. Even in these difficult days, God is watching over you.

It is easy to love the people far away. It is not always easy to love those close to us. It is easier to give a cup of rice to relieve hunger than to relieve the loneliness and pain of someone unloved in our own home. Bring love into your home for this is where our love for each other must start.

Mother Teresa

Standing Strong

God has not given us a spirit of fear and timidity,
but of power, love, and self-discipline.

2 TIMOTHY 1:7 NLT

All of us find our courage tested by the inevitable challenges of life. And when we focus on our fears and our doubts, we find many reasons to lie awake at night and fret about the uncertainties of the future. But here's a better strategy: focus not on your fears but on your God.

Are you willing to trust God, not just when times are good, but also when times are tough? He will be your shield and your strength if you go to Him in faith and trust Him with your life. So the next time you're tempted to accentuate the negative, don't do it. Stand strong and remember that God has not given you a spirit of fear; He gives power and love so you can go on with courage and strength. Trust God's plan and His eternal love for you.

God did away with all my fear.
It was time for someone to stand up—
or in my case, sit down. So I refused to move.
Rosa Parks

The Habit of Forgiveness

*Be even-tempered, content with second place,
quick to forgive an offense. Forgive as quickly
and completely as the Master forgave you.*

COLOSSIANS 3:13 MSG

Have you formed the habit of forgiving everybody (including yourself) as soon as possible? The wise person does just that. But sometimes forgiveness is difficult.

When we've been injured or embarrassed, we feel the urge to strike back and to hurt the ones who have hurt us. But Jesus taught that forgiveness is God's way and that mercy is an integral part of God's plan for our lives. In short, we are commanded to weave the thread of forgiveness into the fabric of our lives.

Have you made forgiveness a high priority? Have you sincerely asked God to forgive you for your unwillingness to forgive others? Have you genuinely prayed that those feelings of hatred and anger might be swept from your heart? If not, do so today . . . it's time to free yourself from the chains of bitterness and regret.

Bitterness imprisons life; love releases it.
Harry Emerson Fosdick

Beyond Blame

Get rid of all bitterness, rage, anger, harsh words, and
slander, as well as all types of malicious behavior.

EPHESIANS 4:31 NLT

To blame others for our own problems is the height of
futility. Yet blaming others is a favorite human past-
time. Why? Because blaming is much easier than fixing, and
criticizing others is so much easier than improving ourselves.
So instead of solving our problems legitimately (by doing the
work required to solve them), we are inclined to fret, to blame,
to criticize, while doing precious little else. When we do, our
problems, quite predictably, remain unsolved. The blame game
is seldom won. God doesn't spend much time helping folks who
spend more time blaming than working.

*The willingness to accept responsibility for one's own
life is the source from which self-respect springs.*
Joan Didion

Richly Blessed

The Lord bless you and keep you; the Lord make
His face shine upon you, and be gracious to you.

NUMBERS 6:24–25 NKJV

Because we have been so richly blessed, we should make thanksgiving a habit, a regular part of our daily routines. But sometimes, amid the demands and obligations of everyday life, we may allow interruptions and distractions to interfere with that time of thanksgiving—and even take away from the time we spend with God.

Have you counted your blessings today? And have you thanked God for them? Just a few of His many gifts include your family, your friends, your talents, your opportunities, your possessions, and the priceless gift of eternal life. What glorious gifts! And your loving heavenly Father is the source of every one of them.

So today, as you go about your duties, remember to pause and give thanks to the Lord. He has blessed you beyond measure.

God is the giver, and we are the receivers. And His richest
gifts are bestowed not upon those who do the greatest things,
but upon those who accept His abundance and His grace.

Hannah Whitall Smith

Trusting God to Guide You

Trust in the Lord with all your heart and lean not on your own understanding; in all your ways acknowledge him, and he will make your paths straight.

PROVERBS 3:5–6 NIV

It's easy to become confused or disoriented by the endless complications and countless distractions of life. After all, the world is brimming with them, and if we're not careful, our thoughts and hearts can be hijacked by the negativity that pervades our troubled society.

If you're confused by the complications of everyday life—or if you're unsure of your next step—lean upon God's promises and lift your prayers to Him. Remember that God is your protector. He will love you forever. You are His child. Open your heart to Him and trust Him to guide you. When you do, God will direct your steps and you will receive His blessings today, tomorrow, and throughout eternity.

God's grand strategy, birthed in His grace toward us in Christ, and nurtured through the obedience of disciplined faith, is to release us into the redeemed life of our heart, knowing it will lead us back to Him even as the North Star guides a ship across the vast unknown surface of the ocean.

John Eldredge

Ultimate Protection

God is striding ahead of you. He's right there
with you. He won't let you down; he won't leave
you. Don't be intimidated. Don't worry.

Deuteronomy 31:8 msg

The world can be a dangerous, unsettling place, but you need not journey through this life alone. God is always with you.

In a world filled with dangers and temptations, God is the ultimate armor. In a world filled with misleading messages, God's Word is the ultimate truth. In a world filled with more frustrations than we can count, God offers the ultimate peace.

God has promised to guide us and to protect us, and He always keeps His promises. Are you willing to trust those promises? Will you accept God's peace and wear God's armor against the dangers of our world? When you do, you'll be empowered to live courageously, knowing that you have the ultimate protection—God's unfailing love for you.

If the Lord be with us, we have no cause of fear. His eye
is upon us, His arm over us, His ear open to our prayer—
His grace sufficient, His promise unchangeable.

John Newton

Waiting for God

The Lord is good to those who wait for Him, to the soul who seeks Him. It is good that one should hope and wait quietly for the salvation of the Lord.

<small>LAMENTATIONS 3:25–26 NKJV</small>

Most of us are impatient for God to grant us the desires of our heart. Usually we know what we want, and we know precisely when we want it—right now, if not sooner. But when God's plans differ from our own, we must trust His infinite wisdom and His infinite love.

As busy men and women living in a fast-paced world, many of us find that waiting quietly for God is difficult. Why? Because we are fallible human beings seeking to live according to our own timetables, not God's. In our better moments, we realize that patience is not only a virtue, but it is also the essence of wisdom and the foundation of trust.

So the next time you find yourself impatient for God to reveal His plans, remember that He loves you and that His timetable is always perfect. And have the wisdom to wait.

Your times are in His hands. He's in charge of the timetable, so wait patiently.
Kay Arthur

God First

Steep your life in God-reality, God-initiative, God-provisions. Don't worry about missing out. You'll find all your everyday human concerns will be met.

MATTHEW 6:33 MSG

One of the surest ways to improve your day is to make God your partner. When you put God first in every aspect of your life, you'll be comforted by the knowledge that His wisdom is the ultimate wisdom and that His plans are the right plans for you. When you put God first, your outlook will change, your priorities will change, and your behaviors will change. And, when you put Him first, you'll experience the genuine peace and lasting comfort that only He can give.

In Exodus 20:3, God instructs us to place no gods before Him. Does God rule your heart? Make certain that the honest answer to this question is a resounding yes.

We are God's children. We are Christians first, and then what we do flows from that.
Benjamin Watson

God's Way: Truth

The godly are directed by honesty.

PROVERBS 11:5 NLT

From the time we are children, we're taught that honesty is the best policy. But sometimes it's difficult for us to be honest with other people, and it can be just as difficult to be honest with ourselves. Even when it's tough to be truthful, we can be comforted by the knowledge that honesty is not just the best policy: it's also God's policy.

When you summon the determination and the courage to be forthright with other folks—and when you are equally honest with yourself—you'll reap the rewards of those efforts. So the next time you're confronted with a situation that offers you the choice between the truth and a lie, choose truth. It's the best way to communicate . . . and the best way to live.

*God doesn't expect you to be perfect,
but he does insist on complete honesty.*
Rick Warren

The Power of Fellowship

*Don't you realize that all of you together are the temple
of God and that the Spirit of God lives in you?*

1 CORINTHIANS 3:16 NLT

Everyone deserves to be part of a community of faith. Fellowship with others can make a powerful contribution to the quality of your own life and to the lives of your loved ones. Communal worship enhances both community and worship.

Are you an active member of a Christian fellowship? Are you a builder of bridges within the four walls of your church and outside it? And do you contribute to God's glory by contributing your time and your talents? The church is intended to be a powerful tool for spreading God's message and uplifting His children. And God intends for you to be a fully contributing member. Your intentions should be the same.

*Be united with other Christians. A wall with loose bricks
is not good. The bricks must be cemented together.*

Corrie ten Boom

The Right Kind of Riches

*Love not the world, neither the things that are in the world. If
any man love the world, the love of the Father is not in him.*

1 JOHN 2:15 KJV

Okay, be honest—are you just a little bit in love with
stuff? Has your pursuit of possessions has left you feeling
empty? If so, you know the painful truth: no matter how much
you love stuff, stuff will not love you back.

Material goods are not nearly as important as we sometimes make them out to be. Of course, we all need the basic
necessities of life; however, once we meet those needs for ourselves and our families, the piling up of possessions often creates more problems than it solves. But God has promised us
riches far beyond those of this world. When we love Him, He
loves us back—and we become rich in spirit.

Martin Luther observed, "Many things I have tried to
grasp and have lost. That which I have placed in God's hands I
still possess." Although our earthly riches are transitory, we can
store up spiritual riches that will last forever.

*When we put people before possessions in our hearts,
we are sowing seeds of enduring satisfaction.*
Beverly LaHaye

Looking for the Good

Make me hear joy and gladness.
PSALM 51:8 NKJV

If you believe in an all-knowing, all-loving God, you'll find it hard to be a pessimist. After all, with God on your side you have every reason to have a positive outlook. Yet you're only human, so from time to time you may fall prey to fear, doubt, or discouragement. If you've been plagued by these negative feelings lately, it's time to lift your hopes . . . and lift a few prayers to God.

Time and again, the Bible reminds us of God's blessings. In response to His grace, let us strive to focus our thoughts on things that are pleasing to Him, not upon things that are corrupting, discouraging, or frustrating.

The next time you find yourself mired in the pit of pessimism, ask God to help you redirect your thoughts. Ask Him to make you hear joy and gladness. This world is God's wonderful creation; when you look to Him and look for the best, you won't have to look far to find it.

There is wisdom in the habit
of looking at the bright side of life.
Father Flanagan

Real Repentance

*I preached that they should repent and turn to God
and prove their repentance by their deeds.*

ACTS 26:20 NIV

Who among us has not sinned? The good news is this:
when we sincerely turn our hearts to God and ask Him
to forgive us, He does forgive—absolutely and completely.

But genuine repentance requires more than simply offering
God apologies for our misdeeds. Real repentance may start
with feelings of sorrow and remorse, but it ends only when we
turn away from the sin that has heretofore distanced us from
our Creator. We offer our most meaningful apologies to God
not with our words, but with our actions. As long as we are still
engaged in wrong behaviors, we may be "repenting," but we
have not fully "repented."

Is some aspect of your life distancing you from God? Real
repentance may not be easy, but you don't have to do even that
much alone. When you ask God to forgive you, ask Him also
to help you to live out your repentance by changing your behavior.
He will be faithful to strengthen you . . . and to draw
you back into His loving arms.

To do so no more is the truest repentance.
Martin Luther

Remaining Humble

*When you do things, do not let selfishness or
pride be your guide. Instead, be humble and give
more honor to others than to yourselves.*

PHILIPPIANS 2:3 NCV

Humility earns rewards that pride will never know. That's why the greatest people are those humble servants who care little for their own glory and choose, instead, to give God the credit He deserves.

Sometimes our faith is tested more by prosperity than by adversity. Why? Because in times of plenty we may be tempted to convince ourselves that we're "self-made" men and women. In truth, all of our gifts flow from the Creator.

Would you like to experience the full measure of God's blessings? To experience the peace and comfort that God gives the most humble of His servants? Then give the Father the full measure of your thanksgiving, with humility in your heart and praise on your lips—starting now.

A man wrapped up in himself makes a very small bundle.
Ben Franklin

Seek, Find, and Ask

If you seek God, your God, you'll be able to find him if you're serious, looking for him with your whole heart and soul.

DEUTERONOMY 4:29 MSG

Where is God? He is everywhere you have ever been and everywhere you will ever go. He is with you night and day; He knows your every thought; He hears your every heartbeat. But sometimes, in the crush of your daily duties, God may seem far away. Or when the disappointments and sorrows of life leave you brokenhearted, you can feel as though God is distant. But He's not. When you earnestly seek God, you will find Him. He wants you to seek Him; He wants to be found by you. He is right here, waiting patiently for you to reach out to Him.

Would you like to experience the comfort, the peace, and the assurance that only God can give? Then send your soul on a quest for God. When you seek Him with all your heart, He will not hide from you; He will show Himself in real and wonderful ways.

Don't take anyone else's word for God. Find Him for yourself, and then you, too, will know, by the wonderful, warm tug on your heartstrings, that He is there for sure.
Billy Graham

Cause to Celebrate

A miserable heart means a miserable life; a cheerful heart fills the day with song.

PROVERBS 15:15 MSG

This day is a precious gift, but it expires at the stroke of midnight. So let us give thanks for these hours on loan from heaven, celebrating them and filling them with song.

God created you in His own image, and He wants you to experience joy and abundance. And He will do His part to ensure that you know spiritual peace and comfort. His love and the life He has given you are ample reason to celebrate. Today, refuse to give in to misery. Choose a cheerful heart, for God has given you plentiful cause for thanksgiving.

You've heard the saying, "Life is what you make it." That means we have a choice. We can choose to have a life full of frustration and fear, but we can just as easily choose one of joy and contentment.
Dennis Swanberg

Refining Your Skills

Do not neglect the spiritual gift within you.

TIMOTHY 4:14 NASB

God has blessed you with an array of talents and opportunities that are uniquely yours. Are you willing to use your gifts in the way God intends? And are you willing to summon the discipline required to develop your talents and to hone your skills? That's precisely what God wants you to do, and that's precisely what you should desire for yourself.

As you seek to expand your talents, you will undoubtedly encounter stumbling blocks along the way—things like fear of rejection or fear of failure. When you do, don't stumble! Take those concerns to God in prayer, and then keep walking in faith, refining your skills and offering your services to God. When the time is right, He will use you—but it's up to you to be thoroughly prepared when He does.

*If you want to reach your potential,
you need to add a strong work ethic to your talent.*
John Maxwell

When You Have Questions

*The counsel of the Lord standeth for ever, the
thoughts of his heart to all generations.*

PSALM 33:11 KJV

When you and your loved ones have questions that you simply can't answer, whom do you ask? When you face difficult decisions, to whom do you turn for counsel? To friends? To mentors? To family members? Or do you turn first to the ultimate source of wisdom? The answers to life's big questions start with God and His Word.

God's wisdom stands forever. God's Word is a light for every generation. Make it your light as well. Use the Bible as a compass for the next stage of your journey. Use it as the yardstick by which your behavior is measured. And as you carefully consult the pages of God's Word, prayerfully ask Him to reveal the wisdom that you need. When you and your family members take your concerns to God, He will not turn you away; He will, instead, offer answers that are tested and true. Your job is to ask, to listen, and to trust.

*Be to the world a sign that while we as Christians
do not have all the answers, we do know
and care about the questions.*
Billy Graham

Planning with God

Careful planning puts you ahead in the long run;
hurry and scurry puts you further behind.

PROVERBS 21:5 MSG

Perhaps you have a clearly defined plan for the future. But even if you don't, rest assured that God does. Your heavenly Father has a definite plan for every aspect of your life. Your role is to sincerely seek God's guidance and to follow the path He gives.

Listening to God can be difficult at times because He often speaks in quieter tones than the world around us. That's why it's so important to carve out solitary moments with Him throughout the day, prayerfully seeking His wisdom and His will.

So as you make preparations for the next stage of your life's journey, be sure to consult the ultimate Source of wisdom. When you allow God to guide your steps—when you allow His plans to become your plans—you'll be blessed indeed.

My policy has always been to ask God to help me set goals
because I believe God has a plan for every person.
Bill Bright

Education Begins at Home

Train up a child in the way he should go, and
when he is old he will not depart from it.

PROVERBS 22:6 NKJV

Here in the twenty-first century, education is no longer a luxury. It is a powerful tool and a shining light that snuffs out the darkness of ignorance and poverty. And when it comes to education, you and your family deserve nothing but the best.

Every child also deserves training in character building: lessons about honesty, responsibility, discipline, attitude, courtesy, dignity, self-worth, and respect for others. Certainly those lessons can and should be taught in school, but the ultimate training ground should be the home.

For grown-ups and kids alike, it's important to remember that school is always in session. So make a commitment to teach the important lessons as soon—and as often—as possible.

The task of the modern educator
is not to cut down jungles but to irrigate deserts.
C. S. Lewis

Unbending Truth

*People with integrity walk safely, but those who
follow crooked paths will slip and fall.*

<small>PROVERBS 10:9 NLT</small>

As thoughtful adults, we know right from wrong. But we
can too easily lose sight of those distinctions in a world
that presents us with countless temptations dressed up in the
robes of faux virtue. These temptations have the potential to
harm us, in part because they lead us to be dishonest with ourselves and with others.

Once we start bending the truth, we're likely to keep
bending it. But if we acquire the habit of being completely
forthright with God, with other people, and with ourselves,
we'll avoid the crooked and slippery path that leads to our
downfall.

The next time you're faced with an opportunity to bend
the truth, choose integrity instead. When you do, your footing
will remain firm and your life will be blessed.

*The greatest friend of truth is time; her greatest enemy
is prejudice, and her constant companion humility.*
Chuck Colson

Mistakes Happen

If we confess our sins to him, he is faithful and just to forgive us our sins and to cleanse us from all wickedness.

1 JOHN 1:9 NLT

Accountant-turned-comedian Bob Newhart became one of America's favorite funnymen by playing bumbling characters plagued by a constant stream of blunders. But in real life, Newhart realized that the little foul-ups usually result in far less drama.

Newhart observed, "It's all right to make mistakes. The whole world isn't depending on you."

If you're quick to beat yourself up over the little mistakes that are an inevitable part of everyday living, perhaps it's time to lighten up. You can't expect perfection from the world, and you shouldn't expect it from yourself, either. Repent; God forgives you, so forgive yourself, too. Today, do your best—and don't worry about the rest. Mistakes happen, but one of the biggest mistakes you can make is torturing yourself when they do.

Success does not consist in never making mistakes but in never making the same one a second time.
George Bernard Shaw

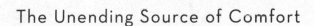

The Unending Source of Comfort

*When doubts filled my mind, your comfort
gave me renewed hope and cheer.*

PSALM 94:19 NLT

Some stages of life are relatively carefree, but in adulthood, we all find that we must endure some difficult days . . . or even some difficult years. In times of adversity, remember the words of Jesus, who, when He walked on the waters, reassured His anxious disciples: "Take courage! It is I. Don't be afraid" (Matthew 14:27 NIV).

We, like the disciples, will have our share of doubts and fears. But because we have God's promise of eternal love and eternal life, we can face those fears with courage and with faith.

Are you facing a difficult challenge? Worried about the future? Struggling with doubt? Take courage and don't be afraid. Take your fears to God and He will replace them with hope and cheer.

We shall be "quiet from the fear of evil," for no threatening of evil can penetrate into the "high tower" of God.
Hannah Whitall Smith

DECEMBER

All Things Possible

All things are possible for the one who believes.

MARK 9:23 NCV

Are you genuinely excited about life and about the opportunities that God has placed before you? Do you think that your Creator is a God of infinite possibilities, and are you energized by that thought? If so, you're a wise person. But if you've been living under a cloud of doubt, or if you're unsure whether or not to be excited about this day (and all the ones that follow it), God wants to have a little chat with you.

God's Word teaches us that all things are possible through Him. Do you believe that? If you do, then you can face the future with a mixture of excitement and delight.

God's power isn't limited, and neither are your possibilities—and the sooner you realize it, the sooner you'll start building a better life for you and your loved ones.

Every intersection on the road of life is an opportunity.
Duke Ellington

Starting to Solve

Are there those among you who are truly wise and understanding? Then they should show it by living right and doing good things with a gentleness that comes from wisdom.

JAMES 3:13 NCV

Are you facing a big job or a particularly difficult task? If so, the most appropriate day to begin tackling that task is today.

Perhaps your challenges are simply too big to solve in a single sitting. But just because you can't solve everything doesn't mean that you should do nothing. Even small, incremental improvements are still improvements. Besides, once you get started solving your problems, you're likely to build momentum. And maybe, just maybe, the task at hand won't turn out to be as daunting as you first feared.

So today, as a favor to yourself and as a way of breaking the bonds of procrastination, do one thing to make your situation better. Even a small step in the right direction is still a step in the right direction. And a small step is far, far better than no step at all.

 You must do the thing you think you cannot do.
Eleanor Roosevelt

Decision Making 101

An indecisive man is unstable in all his ways.

JAMES 1:8 HCSB

When you arrive at one of life's many crossroads, here are some things you can do to help you make those important decisions:

1. Gather as much information as you can.
2. Don't be impulsive.
3. Rely on the advice of trusted friends and mentors.
4. Pray for guidance.
5. Listen to the still, small voice of the Spirit.
6. When the time for action arrives, act. Procrastination is the enemy of progress; don't let it defeat you.

People who can never quite seem to make up their minds often live in a state of discomfort. But when you sincerely seek God and line up your desires with His will, He'll help you to make the right decisions.

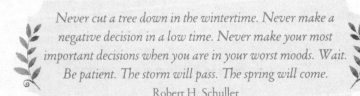

Never cut a tree down in the wintertime. Never make a negative decision in a low time. Never make your most important decisions when you are in your worst moods. Wait. Be patient. The storm will pass. The spring will come.
Robert H. Schuller

When People Behave Badly

Bad temper is contagious—don't get infected.
PROVERBS 22:25 MSG

Sometimes people can be unkind, even rude. When thoughtless people are unkind to you, you may be tempted to strike back, either verbally or in some other way. Don't do it! Instead, remember that God corrects other people's behaviors in His own way, and He doesn't need your help (even if you're totally convinced that He does).

So when other folks behave cruelly, foolishly, or impulsively—as they will from time to time—don't be hotheaded. Don't allow anger to hijack your emotions or your life. Instead, when someone is unkind to you, speak up for yourself as politely as you can and walk away. Forgive those folks as quickly as you can, and leave the rest up to God. When you do, the Creator will bless you with the genuine peace and comfort that are the rewards of people wise enough to forgive.

Forgiveness is not an emotion. . . . Forgiveness is an act of the will, and the will can function regardless of the temperature of the heart.
Corrie ten Boom

Energized for Life

Be energetic in your life of salvation, reverent and
sensitive before God. That energy is God's energy,
an energy deep within you, God himself willing and
working at what will give him the most pleasure.

PHILIPPIANS 2:12–13 MSG

Are you fired up with enthusiasm for life? Are you excited about your work and your calling? Are you accom-
plishing the most important things on your to-do list? If so,
congratulations—keep up the good work!

But if your spiritual batteries are running low, or if you
can't find the strength to get everything done, then perhaps
you're spending too much energy working for yourself and not
enough working for God.

If you're feeling tired or troubled, don't despair. Spend a little time prioritizing your life and be sure to put first things first.
Then seek strength from the Source that never fails. When you
sincerely petition Him, He will give you all the strength you
need to accomplish all the things you really need to do.

*When the dream in our heart is one that God has planted
there, a strange happiness flows into us. . . . Our praying
is then at one with the will of God and becomes a channel
for the Creator's . . . purposes for us and our world.*

Catherine Marshall

Pray Hard, Work Hard

Each tree is known by its own fruit.
LUKE 6:44 HCSB

The old adage is true: we must pray as if everything depended upon God but work as if everything depended upon us. Yet sometimes, when we are weary and discouraged, we may allow our worries to sap our energy and our hope. God has other intentions. God wants us to pray for things, and He wants us to be willing to work for the things that we pray for. More important, God wants our work to become His work.

Are you working hard for your family and for your God? If so, you can expect your heavenly Father to bring forth a rich harvest.

And if you have concerns about the inevitable challenges of everyday living, take those concerns to God in prayer. He will guide your steps, He will steady your hand, He will calm your fears, and He will reward your efforts.

Can anything be sadder than work unfinished? Yes: work never begun.
Christina Rossetti

Looking to Jesus

*This is the secret: Christ lives in you, and this is
your assurance that you will share in his glory.*

Colossians 1:27 nlt

Hannah Whitall Smith spoke to Christians of every generation when she advised, "Keep your face upturned to Christ as the flowers do to the sun. Look, and your soul shall live and grow." When we turn our hearts to Jesus, we receive His blessings, His peace, and His grace.

Jesus belongs at the very center of our lives. And when we put Him there with our thoughts, our prayers, and our deeds, we are blessed. As we look upward to God's Son, we discover a genuine sense of serenity and abundance that the world, by itself, simply cannot provide. So today, share the story of Christ's love with a family member or friend. It's a message that someone very near you desperately needs to hear.

*When you can't see him, trust him.
Jesus is closer than you ever dreamed.*
Max Lucado

Putting Trouble Behind You

If you do nothing in a difficult time, your strength is limited.
PROVERBS 24:10 HCSB

William James was the son of a noted theologian, the brother of a great novelist, a Harvard professor, and one of the founding fathers of American psychology. He was also a commonsense philosopher who once observed, "Nothing is so fatiguing as the eternal hanging on of an uncompleted task."

Sometimes it's tempting to postpone the unpleasant, thus allowing minor problems to mushroom. But as James was quick to point out, procrastination is sand in the machinery of life. So do yourself a favor: finish the unfinished work (even if it's unpleasant) before you begin something else. Because the very best place to put trouble is behind you.

All that is necessary to break the spell of inertia and frustration is this: act as if it were impossible to fail. That is . . . the command of right about face which turns us from failure to success.
Dorothea Brande

The Right to Say No

In a race, everyone runs but only one person gets first prize.... To win the contest you must deny yourselves many things that would keep you from doing your best.

1 CORINTHIANS 9:24–25 TLB

You know all too well how many people are making demands upon your time. If you're like most people, you've got plenty of people pulling you in lots of directions, starting, of course, with your family—but not ending there.

Perhaps you also have additional responsibilities at work or at church. Maybe you're active in community affairs, or maybe you are involved in any of a hundred other activities that gobble up big portions of your day. If so, you'll need to be sure that you know when to say enough is enough.

When it comes to squeezing more and more obligations onto your daily to-do list, you have the right to say no when you simply don't have the time, the energy, or the desire to do the job. And you'll learn to say no as often as necessary.

*Learn to say no gracefully;
resist the temptation to chase after more pleasure,
more hobbies, and more social entanglements.*

James Dobson

Letting Go of the Past

You're familiar with the command to the ancients, "Do not murder." I'm telling you that anyone who is so much as angry with a brother or sister is guilty of murder.

MATTHEW 5:21–22 MSG

Do you invest more time than you should reliving the past or dreaming of revenge? Are you troubled by feelings of anger, bitterness, or regret? If so, it's time to get serious about putting the past in its proper place: behind you.

Perhaps there's something in your past that you deeply regret. Why not make today the day you ask for God's help—sincerely and prayerfully—as you determine, once and for all, to move beyond yesterday's pain so you can fully savor the precious present.

Of course, it's natural to want to lick the wounds of injustices you've suffered and to hold grudges against the people who inflicted them. But God has a better plan: He wants you to live in the present, not the past, because He knows you'll be happier and healthier when you do.

 Don't waste today's time cluttering up tomorrow's opportunities with yesterday's troubles.
Barbara Johnson

DECEMBER 11

The Right Kind of Fear

> The fear of the Lord is the beginning of knowledge,
> but fools despise wisdom and discipline.
>
> PROVERBS 1:7 NIV

Do you have a healthy, fearful respect for God's power? If so, you are wise. And because you are a thoughtful person who has seen their fair share of life, you also understand that genuine wisdom begins with a profound appreciation for God's limitless power.

God praises humility and punishes pride. That's why God's greatest servants will always be those humble men and women who care less for their own glory and more for God's. In God's kingdom, the only way to achieve greatness is to shun it. And the only way to be wise is to understand these facts: God is great, He is all-knowing, and He is all-powerful. We must respect Him, and we must humbly obey His commandments, or we must accept the consequences of our misplaced pride.

> *The fear of God is the death of every other fear.*
> C. H. Spurgeon

God's Love for You

He who does not love does not know God, for God is love.

1 JOHN 4:8 NKJV

God loves you. He loves you more than you can imagine, and His affection is deeper than you can fathom. And as a result of His love, you have an important decision to make. You must decide what to do about God's love: you can return it, or reject it.

When you accept the love that flows from the heart of God, it will transform you. When you embrace God's love, you'll feel different about yourself, your neighbors, your community, your church, and your world. When you open your heart to God's love, you will feel compelled to share God's message—and His compassion—with others. God's heart is overflowing with love for you. Accept it, return it, and share it with someone today.

Love seeks one thing only: the good of the one loved. It leaves all the other secondary effects to take care of themselves. Love, therefore, is its own reward.

Thomas Merton

The God Who Heals

He heals the brokenhearted and bandages their wounds.

PSALM 147:3 NCV

When we suffer heartbreak, it may seem, at least to us, that our hearts can never be repaired. But God knows better. He knows that we can recover, and He promises that when we ask for His help, He will answer our prayers (Luke 11:9–10).

Has your heart been broken? Are you feeling troubled, confused, weak, or sorrowful? If so, please remember that God is not just near; He is right here, right now, trying to get His message of love through to you. So open your heart to the Creator; spend quiet time with Him today (and every day); ask Him to comfort your spirit, heal your heart, and ease your mind. Don't expect healing to be instantaneous, but do expect it to come in time . . . just as God has promised.

A mighty fortress is our God, a bulwark never failing;
Our helper He amid the flood of mortal ills prevailing.
Martin Luther

Focusing on the Future

One thing I do, forgetting those things which are behind and reaching forward to those things which are ahead, I press toward the goal for the prize of the upward call of God in Christ Jesus.

PHILIPPIANS 3:13–14 NKJV

During his thirteen-year tenure at Notre Dame, Knute Rockne gained a permanent and prominent place in football history. His teams enjoyed five undefeated seasons and featured such stars as the "Four Horsemen" and the legendary George Gipp. Rockne advised, "The past is history. Make the present good, and the past will take care of itself." The coach understood that it's tempting to focus on what might have been—tempting, but unproductive.

So if you're looking for a surefire way to improve your tomorrows, let go of yesterday and take firm hold of today. Because you can't change the past, but you can change the future, one day at a time. And today is the best day to start.

*If we open a quarrel between past and present,
we shall find that we have lost the future.*
Winston Churchill

Happiness and Holiness

Happy are the people who live at your Temple. . . .
Happy are those whose strength comes from you.

PSALM 84:4–5 NCV

Do you seek happiness, abundance, and contentment? If so, here are some things you should do: love God; depend on Him for strength; try, to the best of your abilities, to follow His will; and strive to obey His instructions. When you do these things, you'll discover that happiness goes hand in hand with holiness.

The happiest people are not those who struggle against God's will, insisting on their own way; the happiest folks are those who walk with God and trust His guidance.

True happiness is always available—and you need not wait until tomorrow to claim it. So today, focus less on your obstacles and more on God's gifts. Strive, as best you can, to be a genuinely holy person and leave the rest up to God. Then prepare yourself for the blessings—and joys—that are sure to follow.

To be in a state of true grace is to be miserable no more;
it is to be happy forever. A soul in this state is a soul near
and dear to God. . . . It is a soul housed in God.

Thomas Brooks

When We Are Weak, He Is Strong

The God of all grace, who called you to His
eternal glory in Christ Jesus, will personally restore,
establish, strengthen, and support you.

1 PETER 5:10 HCSB

The line from the children's song is both familiar and comforting: "Little ones to Him belong. We are weak, but He is strong." And it's a message that applies to people of all ages: we are all, at times, weak but we worship a mighty God who meets our needs and answers our prayers.

Today, as you encounter the inevitable challenges of daily living, you can turn to God for strength. After all, God's Word promises that you can do all things through Him (Philippians 4:13). The challenge, then, is clear: to place God where He belongs, at the very center of your life. When you do, you will discover that God loves you and He will give you the direction and strength you need. Ask Him to help you today.

*The Lord is the one who travels every mile
of the wilderness way as our leader, cheering us,
supporting and supplying and fortifying us.*
Elisabeth Elliot

The Attitude of a Leader

Those who are wise will shine like the brightness
of the heavens, and those who lead many to
righteousness, like the stars for ever and ever.

DANIEL 12:3 NIV

John Maxwell wrote, "Great leaders understand that the right attitude will set the right atmosphere, which enables the right response from others." If you are in a position of leadership, whether as a parent or as a leader at your workplace, your church, or your school, you can set the right tone by maintaining the right attitude.

Our world needs effective leadership. You can become a trusted, competent, thoughtful leader if you learn to maintain the right attitude—one that's realistic, optimistic, and forward looking. When you do these things, you'll be the kind of leader that others will want to follow.

What I need is someone who will make me do what I can.
Ralph Waldo Emerson

On a Mission for God

You are a chosen people. You are royal priests, a holy
nation, God's very own possession. As a result, you
can show others the goodness of God, for he called
you out of the darkness into his wonderful light.

1 PETER 2:9 NLT

Whether you realize it or not, you are on a personal mission for God. That mission is straightforward: honor God, follow Him, and serve His children.

Of course, you will encounter obstacles as you attempt to discover the exact nature of God's purpose for your life. You must never lose sight of the overriding purposes God has established for all people—that we worship Him sincerely and that we love our neighbors as we love ourselves.

Every day presents opportunities for you to honor God with your words, your prayers, and your service. When you do, you will be blessed in amazing ways. So today, seek God's will, serve people, trust His promises, and enjoy His bountiful rewards.

Without God, life has no purpose,
and without purpose, life has no meaning.
Rick Warren

The Beauty of Your Aspirations

*Commit your works to the Lord, and your
thoughts will be established.*

PROVERBS 16:3 NKJV

Are you nurturing your hopes and dreams in anticipation, or stifling your own dreams before they can even begin? If you're a thoughtful and thankful person, you already have countless reasons to rejoice. But sometimes rejoicing may be the last thing on your mind. At times you may feel overwhelmed by the inevitable stresses or the occasional disappointments of everyday life. But for a thankful person like you, any feelings of discouragement can—indeed, should—be temporary.

The next time you become disheartened by the direction of your day or your life, ask God to help you count your blessings, not your hardships. And while you're talking to God, remember that even when the challenges of the day seem daunting, He remains steadfast. And so must you.

*Far away in the sunshine are my highest aspirations.
I may not reach them, but I can look up and see the beauty,
believe in them, and try to follow where they lead.*
Louisa May Alcott

The Chains of Perfectionism

Those who wait for perfect weather will never plant seeds;
those who look at every cloud will never harvest crops.

ECCLESIASTES 11:4 NCV

There's never a "perfect" time to do anything. That's why we can always find reasons to put off until tomorrow the things we should be doing today.

If you find yourself bound by the chains of perfectionism and procrastination, ask yourself what you're waiting for or, more accurately, what you're afraid of and why. As you examine the emotional roadblocks that have heretofore blocked your path, you may discover that you're waiting for the "perfect" moment, that instant when you feel neither afraid nor anxious. But in truth, perfect moments like these are few and far between.

So stop waiting for the perfect moment and focus, instead, on finding the right moment to do what needs to be done. Then trust God and step out in faith. When you do, you'll discover that with God's help, you can accomplish great things . . . and that you can accomplish them sooner rather than later.

Better to do something imperfectly
than to do nothing flawlessly.
Robert Schuller

God-Prompted Priorities

Seek first God's kingdom and what God wants.
Then all your other needs will be met as well.

MATTHEW 6:33 NCV

Have you asked God for guidance and for the courage to do the things you know need to be done? If you do, then you'll not only be keeping your checklist in check but also inviting God to reveal Himself in various ways as you go about your day.

When you allow God to reign in your heart, He will shower you with spiritual blessings that are too numerous to count and too amazing to anticipate. So as you plan for the day ahead, let God prompt your priorities. It's the surest way to have everything you need to get through your day . . . and your life.

The moment you wake up each morning, all your wishes and hopes for the day rush at you like wild animals. And the first job each morning consists in shoving it all back; in listening to that other voice, taking that other point of view, letting that other, larger, stronger, quieter life come flowing in.

C. S. Lewis

The Blessings of Obedience

It is the Lord your God you must follow, and him you must revere. Keep his commands and obey him; serve him and hold fast to him.

DEUTERONOMY 13:4 NIV

We are sorely tempted to pick and choose which of God's commandments we will obey and which of His commandments we will discard. But God's Word commands us to obey all of His laws, not just the ones that are easy or convenient. When we do, we are blessed by a loving heavenly Father.

Today, take every step of your journey with God as your traveling companion. Read His Word and obey His commandments. Support only those activities that further God's kingdom and your spiritual growth. Be an example of righteous living to your family, to your friends, to your neighbors, and to your community. Then reap the blessings that God has promised to all those who live according to His will and His Word.

Our obedience does not make God bigger or better than He already is. . . . Anything God commands of us is so that our joy may become full—the joy of seeing His glory revealed to us and in us!
Beth Moore

Pleasing Whom?

> Do you think I am trying to make people accept
> me? No, God is the One I am trying to please.
>
> GALATIANS 1:10 NCV

I f you're like most people, you seek the admiration of your
neighbors, your coworkers, and your family members. But
your eagerness to please others should never overshadow your
eagerness to please God. In every aspect of your life, pleasing
your heavenly Father should come first.

Would you like a time-tested formula for successful living—a strategy that will enrich your own life and the lives of
your loved ones? Here is a formula that is proven and true:
seek God's approval first and other people's approval later.
Does this sound too simple? Perhaps it is, but it is also the
surest way to reap the marvelous riches that God has in store
for you and yours.

*When we are set free from the bondage of pleasing
others . . . when we are free from currying others' favor
and others' approval—then no one will be able to
make us miserable or dissatisfied. If we know we have
pleased God, contentment will be our consolation.*
Kay Arthur

Power Supply

Come to Me, all you who are weary and burdened, and I will
give you rest. All of you, take up My yoke and learn from Me,
because I am gentle and humble in heart, and you will find rest
for yourselves. For My yoke is easy and My burden is light.

MATTHEW 11:28–30 HCSB

H ave you been trying to get through life using nothing but
your own resources? If so, it's high time for a power boost.
Are you weary, worried, fretful, or fearful? Turn to a strength
much greater than your own.

You have, at your fingertips, a power supply that never
fails. It is the power that flows from God, and He is always willing to share His strength with you. It's up to you to decide how
much energy you need, and to ask for it. When you do, He will
provide it.

Some days are light and breezy, but other days require
quite a bit of heavy lifting. If the weight you're carrying seems
a little too heavy, don't fret. God can help you carry your load.
So what are you waiting for?

*As a sound may dislodge an avalanche, so the prayer
of faith sets in motion the power of God.*
Lettie Cowman

The Shepherd's Care

*Your righteousness, O God, reaches to the
heavens, you who have done great things.*

PSALM 71:19 NASB

Sometimes life can be difficult indeed. But even during our darkest moments, we're protected by a loving heavenly Father.

When we're worried, God can reassure us; when we're sad, God can comfort us. When our hearts are broken, God can bring healing. So we must lift our thoughts and prayers to Him. When we do, He will hear us and answer our prayers.

It's a truth displayed over and over again in the Bible: whatever our problem, God can handle it. He is our Shepherd, and He has promised to look out for us now and forever. You can trust Him, even on your most difficult days. He has done great things in the past, and the Good Shepherd will do great things in your life if you just follow Him. And why wouldn't you follow? With God at your side, you have nothing to fear.

Cast your cares on God; that anchor holds.
Frank Moore Colby

Following Him Today

*Your old life is dead. Your new life, which is your
real life—even though invisible to spectators—
is with Christ in God. He is your life.*

Colossians 3:3 msg

God's Word is clear: when we genuinely invite Him to reign over our hearts, and when we accept His transforming love, we are forever changed. When we welcome Christ into our hearts, an old life ends and a new way of living—along with a completely new way of viewing the world—begin.

Each morning offers a fresh opportunity to invite Jesus, yet once again, to guide our steps and to rule over our hearts and our days. Each morning presents yet another opportunity to take up His cross and follow in His footsteps. Today, let us rejoice in the new life that is ours through Christ, and let us follow Him, step by step, on the path that He first walked.

*God is not running an antique shop!
He is making all things new!*
Vance Havner

Arguments Lost

Refuse to get involved in inane discussions; they always end up in fights. God's servant must not be argumentative, but a gentle listener and a teacher who keeps cool, working firmly but patiently with those who refuse to obey.

2 TIMOTHY 2:23–24 MSG

When we engage in petty squabbles, our losses usually outpace our gains. When we acquire the unfortunate habit of habitual bickering, we do harm to our friends, to our families, to our coworkers, and to ourselves.

Time and again, God's Word warns us that most arguments are a monumental waste of time, and energy, and life. In Titus, we are warned to refrain from "foolish arguments," and with good reason. Such arguments usually do more for the devil than they do for God.

So the next time you're tempted to engage in a silly squabble, whether inside the four walls of your home or outside them, refrain. When you do, you'll be doing everybody a favor, including yourself.

Argument is the worst sort of conversation.
Jonathan Swift

Changing the Status Quo

You were taught to leave your old self. . . . That old self
becomes worse, because people are fooled by the evil things
they want to do. But you were taught to be made new in
your hearts, to become a new person. That new person is
made to be like God—made to be truly good and holy.

EPHESIANS 4:22–24 NCV

If you're enduring tough times, it's easy to feel stuck. But with
God, you're never really stuck anywhere for long. He is a God
of infinite possibilities.

If you find yourself feeling as if you're mired in quicksand,
stuck in a rut, or trapped in an unfortunate circumstance, abandon the status quo by making the changes that God tells you
are right. After all, in God's glorious kingdom, there should be
no place for people who are dejected, discouraged, or disheartened. God has a far better plan for you, and for your loved
ones, too.

*If God has you in the palm of his hand
and your real life is secure in him, then you can venture
forth—into the places and relationships, the challenges,
the very heart of the storm—and you will be safe there.*
Paula Rinehart

A Series of Choices

*I am offering you life or death, blessings or curses.
Now, choose life! . . . To choose life is to love the
Lord your God, obey him, and stay close to him.*

DEUTERONOMY 30:19–20 NCV

Life is a series of choices. And as a thoughtful person who has been richly blessed by the Creator, you have every reason, and every tool you need, to make wise choices. But sometimes, when the daily grind threatens to grind you up and spit you out, it can seem more convenient to make unwise choices—even choices that are displeasing to God. If you do, you'll forfeit the happiness and comfort that might otherwise have been yours.

So today, as you make the many choices your path presents, ask God to help you choose wisely. When you choose to love God and stay close to Him, he promises life and blessings in return.

*The meaning of life. The wasted years of life.
The poor choices of life. God answers
the mess of life with one word: "grace."*
Max Lucado

Trust Yourself

> They show that in their hearts they
> know what is right and wrong.
>
> ROMANS 2:15 NCV

Are you willing to trust your instincts? God gave you intuition for a very good reason: to use it. But sometimes, especially in times of crisis, it's hard to trust your own instincts because your inner voice—the conscience that resides within you and the intuition that seeks to guide you—can be drowned out by fear, worry, anxiety, or confusion. That's why during times of crisis, you must do whatever it takes to look deep within your own heart.

If you're facing a difficult question or an important decision, your most trusted adviser may very well be that quiet voice within. So when your inner voice starts talking, take careful mental notes. And when in doubt, trust yourself.

There is a balance to be maintained in situations. That balance is the Holy Spirit within us to guide us into the truth of each situation and circumstance in which we find ourselves. He will provide us the wisdom to know when we are to be adaptable and adjustable and when we are to take a firm stand and be immovable.

Joyce Meyer

Courage for the Journey

Since God assured us, "I'll never let you down, never walk off and leave you," we can boldly quote, God is there, ready to help; I'm fearless no matter what.

HEBREWS 13:5–6 MSG

As you take the next step in your life's journey, are you willing to enlist God as your traveling companion? Are you willing to trust Him, to obey Him, to honor Him, and to love Him? Are you willing to consult Him before you make important decisions, not just run to Him after things don't go well? If you can answer these questions with a resounding yes, you will know great peace and comfort all of your days.

Today, as a gift to yourself and your loved ones, summon the courage to follow God. Even if the path seems difficult, even if your heart is fearful, trust your heavenly Father and follow Him. Trust Him with your day and with your life. Do His work, care for His children, and share His good news. Let Him guide your steps. He will never leave you, and He will never lead you astray.

Trusting God completely means having faith that He knows what is best for your life. You expect Him to keep His promises, help you with problems, and do the impossible when necessary.
Rick Warren

NOTES

These pages have been provided for your
personal journaling and meditation.

Notes

....
....
....
....
....
....
....
....
....
....
....
....
....
....
....
....
....
....
....
....
....
....
....
....
....

Notes

....
....
....
....
....
....
....
....
....
....
....
....
....
....
....
....
....
....
....
....
....
....
....
....

Notes

Notes

Notes